Solutions Manual

to accompany

Financial Markets and Corporate Strategy

Second Edition

Mark Grinblatt
University of California, Los Angeles

Sheridan Titman
University of Texas at Austin

Prepared by
Bruce Swensen
Adelphi University

 **McGraw-Hill Irwin**

Boston   Burr Ridge, IL   Dubuque, IA   Madison, WI   New York   San Francisco   St. Louis
Bangkok   Bogotá   Caracas   Kuala Lumpur   Lisbon   London   Madrid   Mexico City
Milan   Montreal   New Delhi   Santiago   Seoul   Singapore   Sydney   Taipei   Toronto

McGraw-Hill Higher Education

A Division of The McGraw-Hill Companies

Solutions Manual to accompany
FINANCIAL MARKETS AND CORPORATE STRATEGY
Mark Grinblatt and Sheridan Titman

Published by McGraw-Hill/Irwin, an imprint of the McGraw-Hill Companies, Inc., 1221 Avenue of the Americas, New York, NY 10020. Copyright © 2002, 1998 by the McGraw-Hill Companies, Inc. All rights reserved.

6 7 8 9 0 QSR/QSR 0 9 8 7 6

ISBN 978-0-07-229434-7
MHID 0-07-229434-5

www.mhhe.com

Contents

CHAPTER 1
RAISING CAPITAL IN FINANCIAL MARKETS

1.1)

It is less expensive to use a rights issue when firms have large-block shareholders who can take up the offer. For example, the United Kingdom equity market is almost entirely an institutional market, and large-block shareholders hold a large percentage of common stocks. The existence of these large institutional shareholders can reduce the costs of rights issues for UK firms. The situation in Switzerland is similar.

1.2)

The exercise price matters in the sense that it can affect the success of the rights offering. Firms usually worry that the stock price will fall below the issue price. Some firms set a low exercise price in order to avoid the possibility of failure.

Since the exercise price does not affect either the real value of the firm or the portion of the asset belonging to any one shareholder, shareholders should be indifferent. However, if some shareholders do not exercise their rights, while other shareholders are granted extra shares, then those receiving extra shares are better off if the exercise price is low.

1.3)

Firms usually like to have a stable long-term relationship with their investment bankers. Consequently, a firm would like to negotiate an underwriting with the investment banker instead of inviting competition for the underwriting. The lower costs of competitive underwritings may be illusory when certain non-financial costs are considered. For example, with a negotiated underwriting, investment bankers are willing to do more marketing beforehand. In a competitive underwriting, the investment banker would be unlikely to prepare to market the issue in advance due to the uncertainty about winning the competitive bid.

1.4)

Benefits: (i) Prohibiting insider trading levels the playing field, protecting small investors, in particular, from being taken advantage of unfairly. (ii) It reduces the uncertainty about motives for trade on the other side, which helps shareholders needing cash unload their shares at more fair prices. This may broaden the number of potential investors for an issue, enhancing the value of securities and lowering the cost of capital to firms. (iii) Insider trading might reduce the incentive for analysts to collect their own information which can then result in less efficient markets.

Costs: The insiders' information will be incorporated into prices more slowly if insiders are not allowed to trade on that information.

1.5)

The per-dollar costs of obtaining public capital decrease as the size of the issue increases. For example, much of the certification required by regulatory agencies and exchanges is the same irrespective of the size of the issue. Thus, it is relatively less expensive to obtain outside capital from the public markets for larger issues than it is for smaller issues.

1.6)

In the United States, the Glass-Steagall Act has prevented banks from serving the functions that they do in Germany and in the United Kingdom. In addition, until recently interstate banking prohibitions protected many banks in the U.S. from competition. These considerations limited the advantage of being a large-sized bank in the United States. Recently, Glass-Steagall restrictions have been loosened and U.S. banks have been consolidating and growing.

CHAPTER 2
DEBT FINANCING

2.1)

The argument is not necessarily valid. There are several agencies that compete in the market providing rating services. If one agency reports false information, customers (bondholders) will turn to other sources of information about the debt. If bondholders no longer trust an agency's ratings then firms will not hire the agency in the future. Therefore, it is in rating agencies' best interest to provide impartial and objective ratings.

Possible tests of an agency's ratings validity:

Test 1: Test whether there is a positive relationship between the fees paid by firms and the bond ratings. If not, then the argument is not necessarily true.

Test 2: Use past data for ratings and bond performance to test whether higher ratings are associated with a lower credit spread and a lower default rate in the long run. If such a relationship exists, then the agency has not had the wrong incentives in the past. We can also make forecasts of default experience and long run credit spread based on past rating, and then determine the size of the forecast error.

2.2)

An increase in competition among underwriters in the Eurobond market could explain this phenomenon. As more investment banks participate, prices decrease, volume increases, and the profits for banks decline to normal (competitive) economic profits.

2.3)

Convertible bonds are a cheap way to finance the firm for two reasons: (1) they can resolve some of the bondholder-stockholder conflicts, which can reduce the premium required by the bondholders; (2) they provide bondholders an option, which may reduce the firm's financing cost in the short run when it needs the funds most but finds it difficult to obtain capital.

Small, growing firms favor convertible debt, because these firms know investors are most worried about adverse selection with small, unknown firms. Convertible bonds can guarantee some fixed payment when the firm does not do well, and can allow early stage investors to benefit from the firm's growth if the firm does well. That's why investors usually require a smaller premium during the early stages when the firm needs funds the most yet has the most severe asymmetric information problems.

2.4)

Lower rated bonds have higher default risk. Also, bonds rated A and above have fairly negligible default risk. However, the slopes of the lines indicate that bonds rated below investment grade at issue which survive without default for at least seven years, have default rates that tend to taper off.

2.5)

    a. Actual/actual: $8\%/2 \times \$100 = \$4.00$

    b. 30/360: $4.00

    c. Actual/365: Last coupon payment was February 15, 1998 (this date is included).

       Actual days: $14 + 31 + 30 + 31 + 30 + 31 + 14 = 181$

       (February has 28 days, August 15, 1998 is not included)

$$\frac{181}{365} \times 8\% \times \$100 = \$3.967$$

    d. Actual/360: $\dfrac{181}{360} \times 8\% \times \$100 = \$4.022$

2.6)

Settlement date: August 1, 1998

Actual number of days between February 15, 1998 and August 15, 1998 is:

$14 + 31 + 30 + 31 + 30 + 31 + 14 = 181$

Actual number of days between February 15, 1998 and August 1, 1998 is:

$14 + 31 + 30 + 31 + 30 + 31 = 167$

    a. Actual/actual: $\left(\dfrac{167}{181}\right) \times 4\% \times \$100 = \$3.691$

    b. 30/360: $\left(\dfrac{16 + 30 \times 5}{180}\right) \times 4\% \times \$100 = \$3.689$

    c. Actual/365: $\dfrac{167}{365} \times 8\% \times \$100 = \$3.660$

    d. Actual/360: $\dfrac{167}{360} \times 8\% \times \$100 = \$3.711$

2.7) [Note to users of the first printing of the second edition: Some of the information required to solve this exercise does not appear in the text. This will be corrected in the second printing.]

The following special rules apply for LIBOR: If the x month maturity date of the LIBOR contract falls on a weekend or a holiday, the actual maturity of the contract is the next business day unless the next business day falls in the month after the weekend day or holiday. In the latter case, the maturity date of the contract is the first business day prior to the weekend day or holiday.

Thus, with the first interest payment, since September 4 is a Saturday, the interest is due on the following Monday (September 6). However, September 6 is the U.S. holiday of Labor Day, so it comes due on September 7. Therefore, there are 187 days of accrued interest.

1st $(9\% + 0.5\%)(187/360) = 4.9347\%$, payment = \$49,347

Likewise, since March 4, 2000 is a Saturday, the interest is due on the following Monday.

2nd $(8.75\% + 0.5\%)(186/360) = 4.7792\%$, payment = \$47,792

Here, Sept. 4, 2000 is a Monday.

3rd $(9.125\% + 0.5\%)(184/360) = 4.9194\%$, payment = $49,194

2.8) [Note to users of the first printing of the second edition: The present value formula and concepts used below to calculate the full price of the bond are discussed in detail in Chapter 9.]

Corporate bond: semiannual coupon 30/360

Coupon rate = 5%

Maturity = November 14, 2020

Yield-to-maturity = 6%

Number of days between June 9, 2001 and November 14, 2001:

$22 + (30 \times 4) + 13 = 155$

$$y = \frac{155}{180} = 0.8611$$

$$\text{Full price on June 9, 2001} = \frac{1}{(1+.03)^{0.8611}}\left[\$2.50 + \sum_{t=2}^{40}\frac{\$2.50}{(1+.03)^{t-1}} + \frac{\$100}{(1+.03)^{39}}\right]$$

So, full price P = $88.8065

$$\text{Accrued interest} = \frac{180-155}{180} \times \$2.50 = \$0.3472$$

Flat price = P − $0.3472 = $88.4593

2.9)

Rate = LIBOR + spread to LIBOR = 6.0% + 0.50% = 6.50%

2.10)

Conversion price (in Euros) = 104.947

Conversion price (in dollars) = 100.00 (approximately)

Conversion rate = 1,000/104.947 = 9.53 shares

Conversion premium = (100.00 − 80.00)/80.00 = 25.0%

To compute the conversion premium using the price specified in Euros, first compute the current market price in Euros, using the exchange rate of (104.947/100) = 1.04947

So, the market price in Euros is (80.00 × 1.04947) = 83.9576

Conversion premium = (104.947 − 83.9576)/83.9576 = 25.0%

CHAPTER 3
EQUITY FINANCING

3.1)

Common shares:	91.2 million shares × 1 vote per share
Class B shares:	25.1 million shares × 10 votes per share
Total:	342.2 million total votes

Wrigleys control (22.1 million + 12.9 million × 10) = 151.1 million votes
Therefore, the Wrigleys control (151.1/342.2) = 44.16% of the votes.

3.2)

There are a number of reasons why underwriters would like to be known for accurate pricing. First, an investment bank known for accurate pricing is likely to attract the better firms as clients. An entrepreneur with a highly valued firm would be attracted to the more accurate investment banker who is more likely to recognize the firm's superior value. On the other hand, an entrepreneur with something to hide might prefer the less accurate investment banker who is less likely to discover the bad news. Second, the more accurate investment banker is less likely to be sued by unhappy investors who buy IPOs that later perform poorly. Third, entrepreneurs may benefit from the information uncovered by the investment banker. Fourth, the secondary market for the IPO may be more liquid if investors believe that the IPO was priced accurately. To promote accuracy, underwriters try to hire the best industry experts as analysts; in addition, the book-building process is designed to elicit from investors as much information as possible in order to minimize surprises in the secondary market.

3.3)

From Exhibit 1.7 we see that the total direct costs of going public are approximately:

8.2% × $75 million =$6.15 million

In addition, the issue is likely to be underpriced by about 10%, implying an indirect cost of $7.5 million and a total transaction cost of $13.65 million.

3.4)

Convertible debt and convertible preferred stock are examples of securities that both pay a guaranteed fixed payment and also provide an additional benefit when the firm's stock price increases.

3.5)

There is a potential conflict. When an investment banker brings a new firm to market, it must investigate the company with due diligence. If, during this investigation, the investment bank uncovers unfavorable information about the firm, the deal is likely to be killed and the investment bank will not receive its fee. This would lessen the incentive to dig too deeply. When the issue does go public, the analysts in the sales and trading sectors of the business may be under some pressure to say good things about the stock in order to ensure the success of the new issue. To some extent, the "Chinese Walls" lessen this problem. However, because of these potential conflicts, an investment banker's reputation is his most valuable asset, and, in most cases, investment bankers are unwilling to risk tarnishing their reputations in order to earn some extra money on any single deal.

3.6) There are several reasons why Internet IPOs may have been substantially underpriced. The two most commonly discussed reasons are:

- Internet IPOs were subject to substantial uncertainty and information asymmetries. The Rock (1986) and the Benveniste and Spindt (1989) arguments discussed in the chapter suggest that increased uncertainty and information asymmetries will lead to greater underpricing.

- The amount of money raised in these Internet IPOs was relatively small; in many cases, less than 10% of the firm was sold at the IPO. As a result, the cost of underpricing was relatively small.

3.7)

The market order is a buy and should therefore be filled at the ask price of 18½. The advantage of a limit order is that, if executed, it may generate a purchase at a price below the 18½ ask price. However, if there is private information in the market and someone knows that the stock is likely to be lower than 18 3/8, the order will be filled. On the other hand, the order will not be filled if the information is that the stock price will soon be higher. So you are more likely to obtain the stock at the lower price only when it is a likely loser. This adverse selection problem (see chapter 19) does not arise with the market order, which is why you pay a higher price for such orders.

CHAPTER 4

THE MATHEMATICS AND STATISTICS OF PORTFOLIOS

4.1)

Since $\bar{r}$ is a constant:

$$E\left[(\tilde{r}-\bar{r})^2\right] = E\left(\tilde{r}^2 - 2\tilde{r}\bar{r} + \bar{r}^2\right) = E\left(\tilde{r}^2\right) - 2E\left(\tilde{r}\bar{r}\right) + E\left(\bar{r}^2\right)$$

$$= E\left(\tilde{r}^2\right) - 2\bar{r}E\left(\tilde{r}\right) + \bar{r}^2 = E\left(\tilde{r}^2\right) - 2\bar{r}\bar{r} + \bar{r}^2 = E\left(\tilde{r}^2\right) - \bar{r}^2$$

4.2)

a)

$$\tilde{R}_p = x\tilde{r}_1 + (1-x)\tilde{r}_2$$

$$\mathrm{var}(\tilde{R}_p) = x^2\,\mathrm{var}(\tilde{r}_1) + (1-x)^2\,\mathrm{var}(\tilde{r}_2) + 2x(1-x)\mathrm{cov}(\tilde{r}_1,\tilde{r}_2) = x^2\sigma_1^2 + (1-x)^2\sigma_2^2 + 2x(1-x)\rho\sigma_1\sigma_2$$

b)

$$\frac{d\,\mathrm{var}(\tilde{R}_p)}{dx} = 2x\sigma_1^2 - 2(1-x)\sigma_2^2 + (2-4x)\rho\sigma_1\sigma_2 = 0$$

$$\left(2\sigma_1^2 + 2\sigma_2^2 - 4\rho\sigma_1\sigma_2\right)x = 2\sigma_2^2 - 2\rho\sigma_1\sigma_2$$

$$x = \frac{\sigma_2^2 - \rho\sigma_1\sigma_2}{\sigma_1^2 + \sigma_2^2 - 2\rho\sigma_1\sigma_2}$$

c)

$$\mathrm{cov}\left(\tilde{R}_p,\tilde{r}_1\right) = \mathrm{cov}\left(x\tilde{r}_1 + (1-x)\tilde{r}_2,\tilde{r}_1\right) = x\,\mathrm{cov}\left(\tilde{r}_1,\tilde{r}_1\right) + (1-x)\mathrm{cov}\left(\tilde{r}_2,\tilde{r}_1\right) = x\sigma_1^2 + (1-x)\rho\sigma_1\sigma_2$$

Substituting for x and simplifying gives:

$$\mathrm{cov}(\tilde{R}_p,\tilde{r}_1) = \frac{\sigma_1^2\sigma_2^2\left(1-\rho^2\right)}{\sigma_1^2 + \sigma_2^2 - 2\rho\sigma_1\sigma_2}$$

Similarly:

$$\mathrm{cov}\left(\tilde{R}_p,\tilde{r}_2\right) = \mathrm{cov}\left(x\tilde{r}_1 + (1-x)\tilde{r}_2,\tilde{r}_2\right) = x\,\mathrm{cov}\left(\tilde{r}_1,\tilde{r}_2\right) + (1-x)\mathrm{cov}\left(\tilde{r}_2,\tilde{r}_2\right) = x\rho\sigma_1\sigma_2 + (1-x)\sigma_2^2$$

$$\mathrm{cov}\left(\tilde{R}_p,\tilde{r}_2\right) = \frac{\sigma_1^2\sigma_2^2\left(1-\rho^2\right)}{\sigma_1^2 + \sigma_2^2 - 2\rho\sigma_1\sigma_2}$$

4.3)

$$E\left(\widetilde{R}_{\text{Gamma}}\right) = \frac{1}{4}(0.24) + \frac{1}{8}(0.08) + \frac{1}{2}(0.04) + \frac{1}{8}(-0.16) = 0.07 = 7\%$$

$$\text{var}\left(\widetilde{R}_{\text{Gamma}}\right) = \frac{1}{4}(0.24 - 0.07)^2 + \frac{1}{8}(0.08 - 0.07)^2$$
$$+ \frac{1}{2}(0.04 - 0.07)^2 + \frac{1}{8}(-0.16 - 0.07)^2$$
$$= 0.0143$$

4.4)

a)

$$\frac{\sigma_A^2}{\sigma_B^2} = q$$

$$\text{var}\left(\widetilde{R}_p\right) = \text{var}\left(x\widetilde{r}_A + (1-x)\widetilde{r}_B\right) = x^2\sigma_A^2 + (1-x)^2\sigma_B^2 + 2x(1-x)\rho\sigma_A\sigma_B = 0$$

For $\rho = -1$:

$$\text{var}(\widetilde{R}_p) = [x^2 q + (1-x)^2 - (2x - 2x^2)\sqrt{q}]\sigma_B^2 = 0$$

$$qx^2 + x^2 - 2x + 1 - 2\sqrt{q}x + 2\sqrt{q}x^2 = 0$$

$$\left(1 + q + 2\sqrt{q}\right)x^2 - 2\left(1 + \sqrt{q}\right)x + 1 = 0$$

$$\left[\left(\sqrt{q} + 1\right)x - 1\right]^2 = 0$$

$$0 < x = \frac{1}{\sqrt{q} + 1} = \frac{\sigma_B}{\sigma_A + \sigma_B} < 1$$

b)

For $\rho = 1$:

$$\text{var}\left(\widetilde{R}_p\right) = [qx^2 + x^2 - 2x + 1 + 2\sqrt{q}x - 2\sqrt{q}x^2]\sigma_B^2 = 0$$

$$\left(1 + q - 2\sqrt{q}\right)x^2 + 2\left(\sqrt{q} - 1\right)x + 1 = 0$$

$$\left[\left(\sqrt{q} - 1\right)x + 1\right]^2 = 0$$

$$x = -\frac{1}{\sqrt{q} - 1} = -\frac{\sigma_B}{\sigma_A - \sigma_B}$$

4.5)

$$r_{IBM} = \frac{104 + 3 - 100}{100} = 7\%$$

$$r_{real\ estate} = \frac{23.5 + 6 - 25}{25} = 18\%$$

$$x_{IBM} = \frac{\$10,000}{\$25,000} = 0.40$$

$$\tilde{R}_p = 0.4 \times 7\% + 0.6 \times 18\% = 13.6\%$$

4.6)

a)

$$r_1 = \frac{115 + 6 - 100}{100} = 21.00\%$$

b)

$$r_2 = \frac{100 + 6 - 115}{115} = -7.83\%$$

c)

Average return per year = [21.00% + (-7.83%)]/2 = 6.585%

4.7)

a)

$$x_{Bond,1} = \frac{\$10,000}{\$18,000} = 0.5556$$

$$\tilde{R}_1 = 0.5556 \times 21.0\% + 0.4444 \times 3.5\% = 13.22\%$$

b)

$$x_{Bond,2} = \frac{\$10,000 \times 1.15}{\$10,000 \times 1.15 + \$8000 \times 1.035} = 0.5814$$

$$\tilde{R}_2 = 0.5814 \times (-7.83\%) + 0.4186 \times (3.00\%) = -3.30\%$$

c)

Average return per year = [13.22% + (-3.30%)]/2 = 4.96%.

4.8)

$$cov(\widetilde{R}_{MVP}, \widetilde{R}_W) = cov(.75\widetilde{R}_W + .25\widetilde{R}_{PUT}, \widetilde{R}_W) = .75\sigma_W^2 + .25\sigma_{W,PUT}$$

$$= .75(.18)^2 + .25(-1)(.18)(.54) = 0$$

$$cov(\widetilde{R}_{MVP}, \widetilde{R}_{PUT}) = cov(.75\widetilde{R}_W + .25\widetilde{R}_{PUT}, \widetilde{R}_{PUT}) = .75\sigma_{W,PUT} + .25\sigma_{PUT}^2$$

$$= .75(-1)(.18)(.54) + .25(.54)^2 = 0$$

So, $cov(\widetilde{R}_{MVP}, \widetilde{R}_W) = cov(\widetilde{R}_{MVP}, \widetilde{R}_{PUT})$

In general:

$$cov(\widetilde{R}_p, \widetilde{R}_W) = cov(x\widetilde{R}_W + (1-x)\widetilde{R}_{PUT}, \widetilde{R}_W)$$

$$= x\sigma_W^2 + (1-x)\sigma_{W,PUT}$$

$$= (x)(.18)^2 + (1-x)(-1)(.18)(.54)$$

$$cov(\widetilde{R}_p, \widetilde{R}_{PUT}) = cov(x\widetilde{R}_W + (1-x)\widetilde{R}_{PUT}, \widetilde{R}_{PUT})$$

$$= x\,cov(\widetilde{R}_W, \widetilde{R}_{PUT}) + (1-x)\sigma^2_{PUT}$$

$$= x(-1)(.18)(.54) + (1-x)(.54)^2$$

Setting these two equations equal to each other:

$x(.18)^2 + (1-x)(-1)(.18)(.54) = x(-1)(.18)(.54) + (1-x)(.54)^2$

$[(.18)^2 + 2(.18)(.54) + (.54)^2]x = (.54)^2 + (.18)(.54)$

$x = 0.3888/0.5184 = 0.75$

4.9)

a)

	(1) E[R]	(2) E[R]
ENT	2.33%	-0.25%
CON	1.67%	-3.75%
PHA	4.00%	9.75%
INS	3.33%	5.00%

b)

	Weight		
ENT	0.30		
CON	0.20		
PHA	0.35		
INS	0.15		
		(1)	(2)
$E[R_{ABCO}]$		2.9333%	3.3375%
$Var[R_{ABCO}]$		0.0003651	0.0003228

4.10)

a)

	(1) E[R]	(2) E[R]
ENT	2.33%	-0.25%
CON	1.67%	-3.75%
PHA	4.00%	9.75%
INS	3.33%	5.00%
PENSION	5.00%	5.00%

b)

	Weight		
ENT	0.133		
CON	0.089		
PHA	0.156		
INS	0.067		
PENSION	0.555		

	(1)	(2)
$E[R_{ABCO}]$	4.0810%	4.2640%
$var[R_{ABCO}]$	0.0000722	0.0000642

4.11)

a)

	(1) E[R]	(2) E[R]
ENT	2.33%	-0.25%
CON	1.67%	-3.75%
PHA	4.00%	9.75%
INS	3.33%	5.00%
DEBT	5.00%	5.00%

	Weight
ENT	0.90
CON	0.60
PHA	1.05
INS	0.45
DEBT	-2.00

	(1)	(2)
$E[R_{ABCO}]$	-1.2000%	0.0125%
$var[R_{ABCO}]$	0.0032855	0.0029052

b)

$E[R_{ABCO}] = 3[\text{old expected return}] - 2(5\%)$

$var[R_{ABCO}] = 9[var(\text{old return})]$

Since the old expected return is less than 5%, ABCO is borrowing at a high rate and investing at a low rate, which lowers expected return. The variance is 9 times larger. As the formula indicates, risk-free borrowing increases variance.

c)

The return in part (a) belongs to ABCO's equity holders. The portfolio analysis here treats equity as a portfolio that is long ABCO's assets and short its debt.

4.12)

a) $\text{var}(r) = E[(r - \bar{r})^2]$ b) $\text{var}(r) = E(r^2) - (\bar{r})^2$

	(i)	(ii)	(i)	(ii)
ENT	0.015756	0.013819	0.016300 - 0.000543	0.013825 - 0.000006
CON	0.023889	0.026719	0.024167 - 0.000279	0.028125 - 0.001406
PHA	0.026867	0.030069	0.028467 - 0.001600	0.039575 - 0.009506
INS	0.008889	0.007500	0.010000 - 0.001109	0.010000 - 0.002500

Except for some errors due to rounding, the two formulas produce the same results.

4.13)

COVARIANCE MATRIX

	ENT	CON	PHA	INS
ENT	0.015756	0.013278	-0.013967	-0.006889
CON		0.023889	-0.025333	-0.014444
PHA			0.026867	0.015333
INS				0.008889

CORRELATION MATRIX

	ENT	CON	PHA	INS
ENT	1.000000	0.684401	-0.678843	-0.582115
CON		1.000000	-0.999971	-0.991241
PHA			1.000000	0.992215
INS				1.000000

4.14)

	INV. (BIL$)	WGT	POOR	AVG.	GOOD	MEAN	VAR	STD. DEV.
ENT	2.40000	0.60000	0.20000	-0.05000	-0.08000	0.02333		
CON	1.60000	0.40000	0.15000	0.10000	-0.20000	0.01667		
FIRM	4.00000		0.18000	0.01000	-0.12800	0.02067	0.015868	0.125966
ENT	1.84615	0.46154	0.20000	-0.05000	-0.08000			
PHA	2.15385	0.53846	-0.10000	-0.05000	0.27000	0.04000		
FIRM	4.00000		0.03846	-0.05000	0.10846	0.03231	0.004204	0.064838

	INV. (BIL$)	WGT	POOR	AVG.	GOOD	MEAN	VAR	STD. DEV.
ENT	2.66667	0.66667	0.20000	-0.05000	-0.08000			
INS	1.33333	0.33333	-0.10000	0.10000	0.10000	0.03333		
FIRM	4.00000		0.10000	0.00000	-0.02000	0.02667	0.002756	0.052494
CON	1.45455	0.36364	0.15000	0.10000	-0.20000			
PHA	2.54545	0.63636	-0.10000	-0.05000	0.27000			
FIRM	4.00000		-0.00909	0.00455	0.09909	0.03152	0.002314	0.048106
CON	2.28571	0.57143	0.15000	0.10000	-0.20000			
INS	1.71429	0.42857	-0.10000	0.10000	0.10000			
FIRM	4.00000		0.04286	0.10000	-0.07143	0.02381	0.005079	0.071270
PHA	2.80000	0.70000	-0.10000	-0.05000	0.27000			
INS	1.20000	0.30000	-0.10000	0.10000	0.10000			
FIRM	4.00000		-0.10000	-0.00500	0.21900	0.03800	0.017885	0.133734

4.15)

Scenario 1:   ENT   0.20   -0.05   -0.08

CON   0.15   0.10   -0.20

min var. port: portfolio = (x)(ENT) + $(1-x)$(CON)

$$\text{var}(P) = x^2\,\sigma^2_{ENT} + (1-x)^2\sigma^2_{CON} + 2x(1-x)\sigma_{ENT,CON}$$

$$= (x^2)(.015756) + (1-x)^2(.023889) + (2x)(1-x)(.013278)$$

$$\frac{d\,\text{var}(P)}{dx} = 2x(.015756) - 2(.023889) + 2x(.023889) + 2(.013278) - 4x(.013278) = 0$$

$$x = \frac{\sigma^2_{CON} - \sigma_{ENT,CON}}{\sigma^2_{ENT} + \sigma^2_{CON} - 2\sigma_{ENT,CON}} = \frac{.023889 - .013278}{.015756 + .023889 - 2(.013278)}$$

$x = 0.81068$

$1-x = 0.18932$

Invest   .81068 ($4 billion) = $3.243 billion in ENT

.18932 ($4 billion) = $0.757 billion in CON

$\text{var}(P) = 0.015287$

Scenario 2 : ENT,PHA

$$x = \frac{\sigma^2_{PHA} - \sigma_{ENT,PHA}}{\sigma^2_{ENT} + \sigma^2_{PHA} - 2\sigma_{ENT,PHA}} = \frac{.026867 - (-.013967)}{.015756 + .026867 - 2(-.013967)}$$

$x = 0.57874$

$1\text{-}x = 0.42126$

Invest   .57874 ($4 billion) = $2.315 billion in ENT

          .42126 ($4 billion) = $1.685 billion in PHA

var(P) = 0.003235

Scenario 3: ENT,INS

$$x = \frac{\sigma^2_{INS} - \sigma_{ENT,INS}}{\sigma^2_{ENT} + \sigma^2_{INS} - 2\sigma_{ENT,INS}} = \frac{.008889 - (-.006889)}{.015756 + .008889 - 2(-.006889)}$$

$x = 0.41064$

$1 - x = 0.58936$

Invest   .41064 ($4 billion) = $1.643 billion in ENT

          .58936 ($4 billion) = $2.357 billion in INS

var(P) = 0.002410

Scenario 4: CON,PHA

$$x = \frac{\sigma^2_{PHA} - \sigma_{CON,PHA}}{\sigma^2_{CON} + \sigma^2_{PHA} - 2\sigma_{CON,PHA}} = \frac{.026867 - (-.025333)}{.023889 + .026867 - 2(-.025333))}$$

$x = 0.51468$

$1\text{-}x = 0.48532$

Invest   .51468 ($4 billion) = $2.059 billion in CON

          .48532 ($4 billion) = $1.941 billion in PHA

var(P) = 0.000001

Scenario 5: CON,INS

$$x = \frac{\sigma^2_{INS} - \sigma_{CON,INS}}{\sigma^2_{CON} + \sigma^2_{INS} - 2\sigma_{CON,INS}} = \frac{.008889 - (-.014444)}{.023889 + .008889 - 2(-.014444)}$$

$x = 0.37831$

$1\text{-}x = 0.62169$

Invest   .37831 ($4 billion) = $1.513 billion in CON

          .62169 ($4 billion) = $2.487 billion in INS

var(P) = 0.000060

Scenario 6: PHA,INS

$$x = \frac{\sigma_{INS}^2 - \sigma_{PHA,INS}}{\sigma_{PHA}^2 + \sigma_{INS}^2 - 2\sigma_{PHA,INS}} = \frac{.008889 - .015333}{.026867 + .008889 - 2(.015333)}$$

$x = -1.26601$

$1 - x = 2.26601$

However, since there is no short selling:

let $x = 0$ so that:

$var(P) = \sigma_{INS}^2 = .008889$

4.16)

	Scenario 1			Scenario 2	
	MEAN	STD.DEV		MEAN	STD.DEV.
ENT	2.33%	0.1255	ENT	2.33%	0.1255
CON	1.67%	0.1546	PHA	4.00%	0.1639
50/50	2.00%	0.1286	50/50	3.17%	0.0606
Min.Var.	2.21%	0.1236	Min.Var.	3.03%	0.0569

	Scenario 3			Scenario 4	
	MEAN	STD.DEV		MEAN	STD.DEV.
ENT	2.33%	0.1255	CON	1.67%	0.1546
INS	3.33%	0.0943	PHA	4.00%	0.1639
50/50	2.83%	0.0521	50/50	2.84%	0.0047
Min.Var.	2.92%	0.0491	Min.Var.	2.80%	0.0008

	Scenario 5			Scenario 6	
	MEAN	STD.DEV		MEAN	STD.DEV.
CON	1.67%	0.1546	PHA	4.00%	0.1639
INS	3.33%	0.0943	INS	3.33%	0.0943
50/50	2.50%	0.0312	50/50	3.67%	0.1289
Min.Var.	2.70%	0.0077	Min.Var.	3.33%	0.0943

4.17)

If short sales are permitted, then, for Scenario 6, the minimum variance portfolio has the proportions (from Exercise 4.15):

$x = -1.26601$ and $(1-x) = 2.26601$

The mean return for this portfolio is:

$(-1.26601)(.0400) + (2.26601)(.0333) = .0248 = 2.48\%$

The variance is:

$\text{var}(P) = x^2 \sigma^2_{PHA} + (1-x)^2 \sigma^2_{INS} + 2x(1-x)\sigma_{PHA,INS}$

$\quad = (-1.26601^2)(0.026867) + (2.26601^2)(0.008889) + (2)(-1.26601)(2.26601)(0.015333)$

$\quad = 0.000731$

4.18)

a)

$\text{var}(\widetilde{R}_p) = (0.75^2)(0.03) = 0.016875$

$\sigma_p = 0.1299$

portfolio weights:

$x_1 = \frac{1}{3}(0.75) = \frac{1}{4}, \; x_2 = \frac{1}{6}(0.75) = \frac{1}{8}, \; x_3 = \frac{1}{2}(0.75) = \frac{3}{8}, \; x_4 = \frac{1}{4}$

b)

$\text{var}(\widetilde{R}_p) = (1.5^2)(0.03) = 0.067500$

$\sigma_p = 0.2598$

portfolio weights:

$x_1 = \frac{1}{3} \times 1.5 = 0.5, \; x_2 = \frac{1}{6} \times 1.5 = 0.25, \; x_3 = \frac{1}{2} \times 1.5 = 0.75, \; x_4 = -0.5$

4.19)

Inverse of Covariance Matrix

	Nike	Cisco	GE	SUM	Min. Var. Port. Weights
Nike	875	-375	125	625	0.7142857
Cisco	-375	-125	375	-125	-0.1428571
GE	125	375	-125	375	0.4285714
TOTAL				875	

The weights were obtained by dividing each of the entries in the SUM column by the total, 875.

4.20)

The mean-standard deviation diagram for two risky securities with arbitrary correlation will look like Exhibit 4.5, with the lines extended beyond the endpoints.

4.21)

The estimate of the expected return is the mean of the historical returns:

$(0.3055 + 0.0767 + 0.0999 + 0.0131 + 0.3743)/5 = 0.1739 = 17.39\%$

The variance is computed by first subtracting the mean from each of the five historical returns, to compute the demeaned returns, which are, respectively:

13.16%, -9.72%, -7.40%, -16.08%, 20.04%

The variance is the average squared demeaned return:

$$\frac{(0.1316^2) + (-0.0972^2) + (-0.0740^2) + (-0.1608^2) + (0.2004^2)}{5} = 0.0197$$

4.22)

The weights for the portfolio are:

$x_1 = (\$500/\$2000) = 0.250$, $x_2 = (\$1250/\$2000) = 0.625$, $x_3 = (\$250/\$2000) = 0.125$

In the good economic environment, the mean return of the portfolio is:

$x_1 r_1 + x_2 r_2 + x_3 r_3 = (0.250 \times 0.13) + (0.625 \times 0.06) + (0.125 \times -0.07) = 0.06125 = 6.125\%$

In the bad economic environment, the mean return of the portfolio is:

$x_1 r_1 + x_2 r_2 + x_3 r_3 = (0.250 \times -0.20) + (0.625 \times 0.036) + (0.125 \times 0.02) = -0.02875 = -2.875\%$

The expected return for the portfolio is the weighted average of the portfolio returns in the good and bad economic environments:

$(2/3)(0.06125) + (1/3)(-0.02875) = 0.03125 = 3.125\%$

The variance for the portfolio is:

$(2/3)(0.06125 - 0.03125)^2 + (1/3)(-0.02875 - 0.03125)^2 = 0.00180$

Adding a \$1,000 investment in stock 4 to the portfolio means that the weights for the old portfolio and for stock 4 are, respectively, ($2000/$3000) = 2/3 and ($1000/$3000) = 1/3. Therefore, the return for the new portfolio is:

$(2/3)(0.03125) + (1/3)(0.04000) = 0.03417 = 3.417\%$

Since stock 4 is uncorrelated with the old portfolio, the variance for the new portfolio can be computed as follows:

$(2/3)^2 (0.0018) + (1/3)^2 (0.0200) = 0.003022$

4.23)

The formula for the variance of a portfolio of four assets is:

$$\sigma_p^2 = x_1^2\sigma_1^2 + x_2^2\sigma_2^2 + x_3^2\sigma_3^2 + x_4^2\sigma_4^2$$

$$+ 2x_1x_2\sigma_{12} + 2x_1x_3\sigma_{13} + 2x_1x_4\sigma_{14} + 2x_2x_3\sigma_{23} + 2x_2x_4\sigma_{24} + 2x_3x_4\sigma_{34}$$

Substituting the values for the four assets:

$$\sigma_p^2 = (1/6)^2\,(0.0220) + (1/3)^2\,(0.0517) + (1/4)^2\,(0.0342) + (1/4)^2\,(0.0290)$$

$$+ (1/6)(1/3)\,(0.0093) + (1/6)(1/4)(0.0191) + (1/6)(1/4)(0.0181) + (1/3)(1/4)(0.0120)$$

$$+ (1/3)(1/4)(0.0096) + (1/4)(1/4)(0.0204) = 0.020589$$

Note that the portfolio variance can also be computed using the Excel function MMULT that computes the product of two matrices. Using MMULT, pre-multiply the row of portfolio weights times the 4×4 covariance matrix and then post-multiply by the column of portfolio weights.

5.1) a), b), c), d)

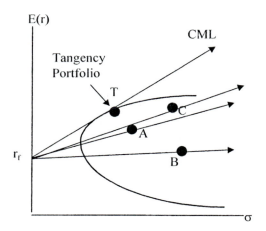

The CML lies above all other lines connecting any risky portfolio with the risk-free asset. One can always find a combination of portfolio T and the risk-free asset that has higher mean and lower standard deviation than any given combination of other portfolios and the risk-free asset. The CML is at least as steeply sloped as any combination of a risk-free asset with any risky investment or portfolio.

e) At the tangency portfolio:

$$\frac{\overline{R}_T - r_f}{\sigma_T^2} = \frac{\overline{r}_i - r_f}{\mathrm{cov}(\widetilde{r}_i, \widetilde{R}_T)} = \frac{\overline{r}_j - r_f}{\mathrm{cov}(\widetilde{r}_j, \widetilde{R}_T)} \quad \text{for all risky assets i and j.}$$

5.2)

Step 1:

$$0.002x_1 + 0.001x_2 + 0x_3 = 0.15 - 0.05 = 0.10$$
$$0.001x_1 + 0.002x_2 + 0.001x_3 = 0.12 - 0.05 = 0.07$$
$$0x_1 + 0.001x_2 + 0.002x_3 = .010 - 0.05 = 0.05$$

The first and third equations simplify to

$$x_1 = 50 - 0.5x_2$$
$$x_3 = 25 - 0.5x_2$$

Substituting these values for x_1 and x_3 in the second equation implies:

$$0.001(50 - 0.5x_2) + 0.002x_2 + 0.001(25 - 0.5x_2) = 0.07$$
$$(-0.0005 + 0.002 - 0.0005)x_2 = 0.07 - 0.050 - 0.025$$
$$x_2 = -5$$

This implies that :

$$x_1 = 50 - 0.5(-5) = 52.5$$
$$x_3 = 25 - .5(-5) = 27.5$$

Step 2: Rescale, so that the weights sum to one:

$$x_1 = 0.7000$$
$$x_2 = -0.0667$$
$$x_3 = 0.3667$$

5.3)

If $r_f = 3\%$:

$$0.002x_1 + 0.001x_2 + 0x_3 = 0.15 - 0.03 = 0.12$$
$$0.001x_1 + 0.002x_2 + 0.001x_3 = 0.12 - 0.03 = 0.09$$
$$0x_1 + 0.001x_2 + 0.002x_3 = 0.10 - 0.03 = 0.07$$

$$x_1 = 60 - 0.5x_2$$
$$x_3 = 35 - 0.5x_2$$
$$0.001(60 - 0.5x_2) + 0.002x_2 + 0.001(35 - 0.5x_2) = 0.09$$
$$60 - 0.5x_2 + 2x_2 + 35 - 0.5x_2 = 90$$
$$95 + x_2 = 90$$
$$x_2 = -5$$
$$x_1 = 62.5$$
$$x_3 = 37.5$$

Rescale:

$$x_1 = 0.6579$$
$$x_2 = -0.0526$$
$$x_3 = 0.3947$$

If $r_f = 7\%$:

$$0.002x_1 + 0.001x_2 + 0 = 0.08$$
$$0.001x_1 + 0.002x_2 + 0.001x_3 = 0.05$$
$$0 + 0.001x_2 + 0.002x_3 = 0.03$$

$$0.002x_1 = 0.08 - 0.001x_2$$
$$x_1 = 40 - 0.5x_2$$

$$0.002x_3 = 0.03 - 0.001x_2$$
$$x_3 = 15 - 0.5x_2$$

$$0.001(40 - 0.5x_2) + 0.002x_2 + 0.001(15 - 0.5x_2) = 0.05$$
$$40 - 0.5x_2 + 2x_2 + 15 - 0.5x_2 = 50$$
$$x_2 = -5$$
$$x_1 = 42.5$$
$$x_3 = 17.5$$

Rescale:

$$x_1 = 0.7727$$
$$x_2 = -0.0909$$
$$x_3 = 0.3182$$

5.4)

	E[R]	σ
AOL	15.00%	4.472%
Microsoft	12.00%	4.472%
Intel	10.00%	4.472%
A: Portfolio ($r_f = 5\%$)	13.37%	3.340%
B: Portfolio ($r_f = 3\%$)	13.18%	3.274%
C: Portfolio ($r_f = 7\%$)	13.68%	3.485%

$E[R_{p1}] = (0.70)(.15) - (0.0667)(.12) + (0.3667)(.10) = 13.37\%$

$\sigma_{p1} = [(0.70^2)(0.002) + (0.0667^2)(0.002) + (0.3667^2)(0.002) + 2(0.70)(-0.0667)(0.001)$
$\qquad + 2(-0.0667)(0.3667)(0.001)]^{1/2} = 3.340\%$

$E[R_{p2}] = (0.6579)(.15) - (0.0526)(.12) + (0.3947)(.10) = 13.18\%$

$\sigma_{p2} = [(0.6579^2)(0.002) + (0.0526^2)(0.002) + (0.3947^2)(0.002) + 2(0.6579)(-0.0526)(0.001)$
$\qquad + 2(-0.0526)(0.3947)(0.001)]^{1/2} = 3.274\%$

$E[R_{p3}] = (0.7727)(.15) - (0.0909)(.12) + (0.3182)(.10) = 13.68\%$

$\sigma_{p3} = [(0.7727^2)(0.002) + (0.0909^2)(0.002) + (0.3182^2)(0.002) + 2(0.7727)(-0.0909)(0.001)$
$\qquad + 2(0.0909)(0.3182)(0.001)]^{1/2} = 3.485\%$

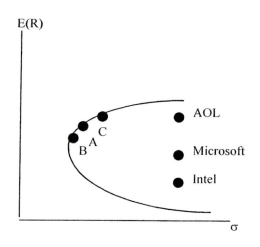

E(R)

AOL

Microsoft

Intel

σ

5.5)

Equally-weighted portfolio:

$E(R_p) = (1/3)(.15) + (1/3)(0.12) + (1/3)(0.10) = 0.1233 = 12.33\%$

$var(R_p) = (1/3)^2(0.002) + (1/3)^2(0.002) + (1/3)^2(0.002) + 2(1/3)^2(0.001) + 2(1/3)^2(0.001)$

$= 0.00111$

$\sigma_p = 3.332\%$

Try adding a little bit of AOL, financing it with an equal sized short position in Microsoft. Since the mean return of AOL (15%) exceeds that of Microsoft (12%), the mean return of the portfolio is increased. However, the equally-weighted portfolio has a lower covariance with AOL than it does with Microsoft, so the variance is decreased. For example, a portfolio with weights of .35 on AOL, .32 on Microsoft, and .33 on Intel, has a mean return of 12.39%, but a variance of 0.00110.

Therefore, the equally-weighted portfolio can be improved upon (in this case by adding AOL and shorting Microsoft). Many other solutions are possible.

5.6)

	Covariance Matrix			Risk Premiums for r_f equal to:		
	AOL	Microsoft	Intel	5%	3%	7%
AOL	0.002	0.001	0.000	0.10	0.12	0.08
Microsoft	0.001	0.002	0.001	0.07	0.09	0.05
Intel	0.000	0.001	0.002	0.05	0.07	0.03

Inverted Covariance Matrix			
	AOL	Microsoft	Intel
AOL	750	-500	250
Microsoft	-500	1000	-500
Intel	250	-500	750

	$r_f = 5\%$		$r_f = 3\%$		$r_f = 7\%$	
	sum	rescale	sum	rescale	sum	rescale
AOL	52.5	0.7000	62.5	0.6579	42.5	0.7727
Microsoft	-5.0	-0.0667	-5.0	-0.0526	-5.0	-0.0909
Intel	27.5	0.3667	37.5	0.3947	17.5	0.3182
TOTAL	75.0	1.0000	95.0	1.0000	55.0	1.0000

5.7)

   a)

$$\beta_i = \frac{\sigma_{iT}}{\sigma_T^2}$$

$\text{cov}(\text{AOL}, T) = (0.7000)(0.002) + (-0.0667)(0.001) + (0.3667)(0) = 0.001333$

$\text{cov}(\text{Microsoft}, T) = (0.7000)(0.001) + (-0.0667)(0.002) + (0.3667)(0.001) = 0.000933$

$\text{cov}(\text{Intel}, T) = (0.7000)(0) + (-0.0667)(0.001) + (0.3667)(0.002) = .000667$

$\sigma_T^2 = 0.001115 = (0.7000)^2(0.002) + (-0.0667)^2(0.002) + (.3667)^2(0.002)$
$\quad\quad - 2(0.7000)(-0.0667)(0.001) + 2(-0.0667)(0.3667)(0.001) = 0.001116$

$$\beta_{\text{AOL}} = \frac{0.001333}{0.001116} = 1.194$$

$$\beta_{\text{Microsoft}} = \frac{0.000933}{0.001116} = 0.836$$

$$\beta_{\text{Intel}} = \frac{0.000667}{0.001116} = 0.598$$

   b)

β of equally-weighted portfolio:

$$\beta = (\tfrac{1}{3})(1.194) + (\tfrac{1}{3})(0.836) + (\tfrac{1}{3})(0.598) = 0.876$$

5.8)

   a)

The boundary portfolio that is uncorrelated with the tangency portfolio satisfies:

$$\text{cov}(x_1 r_1 + x_2 r_2 + (1 - x_1 - x_2) r_3, 0.7r - 0.0667 r_2 + 0.3667 r_3) = 0$$

Minimum variance portfolio (V):

$$\left. \begin{array}{l} 0.002 x_1 + 0.001 x_2 + 0 x_3 = \text{constant} \\ 0.001 x_1 + 0.002 x_2 + 0.001 x_3 = \text{constant} \\ 0 x_1 + 0.001 x_2 + 0.002 x_3 = \text{constant} \end{array} \right\} \Rightarrow \begin{array}{l} x_1 = 0.5 \\ x_2 = 0 \\ x_3 = 0.5 \end{array}$$

This portfolio has a variance of 0.001

Every boundary portfolio can be generated by a combination of the tangency portfolio (T) and the minimum variance portfolio (V). Thus:

$$cov(wr_V + (1-w)r_T, r_T) = 0$$
$$= w\sigma_{V,T} + (1-w)\sigma_T^2 = 0$$
$$= w\sigma_{V,T} + (1-w)(0.001116) = 0$$
$$= w(\sigma_{V,T} - 0.001116) = -0.001116$$

However, $\sigma_{V,T} = \sigma_{V,V} = 0.001$ implying:

$$w = \frac{-0.001116}{0.001 - 0.001116} = 9.621$$

Uncorrelated boundary portfolio:

$$x_1 = w(0.5) + (1-w)(0.7000) = -1.22$$
$$x_2 = w(0) + (1-w)(-0.0667) = 0.57$$
$$x_3 = w(0.5) + (1-w)(0.3667) = 1.65$$

b)

All inefficient portfolios with the same mean as in (a) have the same covariance with the tangency portfolio, i.e., cov=0.

5.9)

The covariance of the return of all portfolios with the same expected return as AOL with the tangency portfolio is the same as the covariance of the return of AOL with the tangency portfolio. This result is from the risk-expected return equation.

$$\underbrace{\overline{r_i}}_{same} - \underbrace{r_f}_{constant} = \beta_i \left(\underbrace{\overline{R_T} - r_f}_{constant} \right)$$

So it must be true that:

$\beta_i = \beta_{Netscape}$ for all i with the same mean.

$$\Rightarrow \beta_i = \frac{cov(r_i, R_T)}{var(R_T)} = \beta_{AOL}$$

or $cov(r_i, R_T) = \beta_{AOL} \, var(R_T)$

$\Rightarrow$ The covariances are all the same (if the portfolios have the same mean).

Since $cov(\tilde{r}_{AOL}, \tilde{R}_T) = 0.00133$

$\Rightarrow$ All portfolios with the same mean as AOL have covariances with the tangency portfolio equal to 0.00133

5.10)

Covariance Matrix

	Apple	Bell South	Caterpillar	Mean return	Risk premium at $r_f = 5\%$
Apple	0.0400	0.0480	-0.0050	0.15	0.10
Bell South	0.0480	0.0900	0.0150	0.10	0.05
Caterpillar	-0.0050	0.0150	0.0625	0.12	0.07

Inverted Covariance Matrix

	Apple	Bell South	Caterpillar	Sum	Minimum Variance Portfolio
Apple	86.33094	-49.16067	18.70504	55.87531	0.94947
Bell South	-49.16067	39.56835	-13.42926	-23.02158	-0.39120
Caterpillar	18.70504	-13.42926	20.71942	25.99520	0.44173
TOTAL				58.84893	1.00000

Inverted Covariance Matrix

	Apple	Bell South	Caterpillar	Risk Premium Weighted Sum	Tangency Portfolio
Apple	86.33094	-49.16067	18.70504	7.48441	1.19634
Bell South	-49.16067	39.56835	-13.42926	-3.87770	-0.61983
Caterpillar	18.70504	-13.42926	20.71942	2.64940	0.42349
TOTAL				6.25611	1.00000

5.11)

a)

$$\overline{R}_A = \frac{6}{6+4}(0.06) + \frac{4}{6+4}(0.12) = 0.0840 = 8.40\%$$

$$\beta_A = \frac{4}{6+4}(0.9) = 0.36$$

$$\sigma_A = \frac{4}{6+4}(0.30) = 0.120$$

b)

If the CAPM holds:

$$\bar{r}_E - r_f = \beta_E \left(\bar{R}_M - r_f \right)$$

$$\bar{R}_M = \frac{\bar{r}_E - r_f}{\beta_E} + r_f = \frac{0.12 - 0.06}{0.9} + 0.06 = 0.1267 = 12.67\%$$

c)

$$\bar{R}_A = \frac{6}{10}(0.07) + \frac{4}{10}(0.12) = 0.0900 = 9.00\%$$

$$\beta_A = \frac{6}{10}(0.2) + \frac{4}{10}(0.9) = 0.48$$

$$\text{var}(\tilde{R}_A) = (0.6)^2 (0.10)^2 + (0.4)^2 (0.30)^2 + 2(0.6)(0.4)(0.009) = 0.02232$$

$$\sigma_A = 0.149$$

5.12)

$$\beta_{EXXON} = 1.09$$

Adjusted $\beta = 0.66\beta_{EXXON} + 0.34 = 1.06$

5.13)

The ratio of the risk premium of the ACYOU Corporation to its covariance with portfolio P must be the same as the comparable ratio for the ACME Corporation.

$$(\bar{r}_{ACME} - r_f)/\text{cov}(\tilde{r}_{ACME}, \tilde{R}_p) = (.20 - .10)/.001 = 100$$

In order for the ACYOU Corporation to have an identical ratio, its expected return must satisfy:

$$(\bar{r}_{ACYOU} - r_f)/\text{cov}(\tilde{r}_{ACYOU}, \tilde{R}_p) = (\bar{r}_{ACYOU} - .10)/.002 = 100$$

This ratio is satisfied if the ACYOU Corporation has an expected return of 30% per year, rather than the 40% per year value specified in Example 5.4.

5.14)

Using the Capital Asset Pricing Model, compute the expected return as follows:

$$\bar{r} = r_f + \beta(\bar{R}_M - r_f) = 0.05 + (0.54)(0.13 - 0.05) = 0.0932 = 9.32\%$$

5.15)

The beta for this portfolio is a weighted average of the betas for the two assets comprising this portfolio:

$$(0.5)(0.54) + (0.5)(1.0) = 0.77$$

5.16)

a)

For the period 1991 to 1995, the average quarterly return for Dell is 14.0565%, so that the annualized expected return is 56.23%.

b)

For the S&P 500, the average quarterly return is 3.2590% and the annualized expected return is 13.04%. The market risk premium is $(13.04\% - 4.9\%) = 8.14\%$ and the beta for Dell over the five year period is 1.935, so that the expected return for Dell can be estimated from the CAPM as follows:

$$\bar{r} = r_f + \beta(\bar{R}_M - r_f) = 0.049 + (1.935)(0.0814) = 0.2065 = 20.65\%$$

The expected return estimated by averaging the quarterly returns results in an estimate of 56.23% when using five years of data, as above, and an estimate of 94.54% when using ten years of data, as in Example 5.9. The expected return estimates obtained by using the risk-expected return equation differ much less: 20.65% (five years of data) and 21.3% (ten years of data). Estimates of required return obtained by averaging historical returns are not very precise and therefore tend to vary more. Estimates based on beta and the risk-expected return equation tend to be much closer to one another and tend to be more representative of the true required rate of return.

5.17)

The Bloomberg adjustment uses the following formula:

Adjusted beta = $(0.66 \times$ Unadjusted beta$) + 0.34$

Using the adjustment formula, the adjusted betas are:

	Unadjusted Beta	Adjusted Beta
Delta Air Lines	0.84	0.89
Procter & Gamble	1.40	1.26
Coca-Cola	0.88	0.92
Gilette	0.90	0.93
Citigroup	1.32	1.21
Caterpillar	1.00	1.00
ExxonMobil	0.64	0.76

5.18)

From Result 5.3, it must be true for the tangency portfolio that the ratio of the risk premium of each stock to its covariance with the tangency portfolio is constant. If we let x represent the weight for Nike, so that $(1 - x)$ is the weight for McDonald's, then, by Result 5.3, the following must be true:

$$\frac{0.15 - 0.06}{(x)(0.04) + (1-x)(0.02)} = \frac{0.14 - 0.06}{(x)(0.02) = (1-x)(0.08)}$$

Solving this equation, the weights are: $x = 0.8$ and $(1 - x) = 0.2$ for the tangency portfolio.

From Result 4.10, the minimum variance portfolio has an equal covariance with the return for every stock in the portfolio. Using this result, the minimum variance portfolio must be the solution to the following equation:

$$(x)(0.04) + (1 - x)(0.02) = (x)(0.02) + (1 - x)(0.08)$$

Solving this equation, the weights are: $x = 0.75$ and $(1 - x) = 0.25$ for the minimum variance portfolio.

5.19)

From Result 5.3, we know that, for the tangency portfolio, the ratio of the risk premium of each stock to its covariance with the tangency portfolio is constant. For Stock I, this ratio is:

$$(0.09 - 0.05)/0.004 = 10.0$$

For Stock II, the ratio is:

$$(0.12 - 0.05)/0.005 = 14.0$$

Since these ratios are not equal, then Portfolio P can not be the tangency portfolio.

5.20)

a)

$$\beta_i = \frac{\text{cov}(r_i, R_T)}{\text{var}(R_T)}$$

$$\beta_{MICROSOFT} = \frac{0.10}{0.25^2} = 1.60$$

b)

$$\overline{r} = r_f + \beta(\overline{R}_M - r_f) = 0.06 + (1.60)(0.16 - 0.06) = 0.220 = 22.0\%$$

c)

Solve for β_{INTEL} in the following equation:

$$\overline{r} = r_f + \beta_{INTEL}(\overline{R}_M - r_f)$$
$$0.11 = 0.06 + \beta_{INTEL}(0.16 - 0.06)$$

$$\beta_{INTEL} = 0.50$$

d)

The beta of the portfolio is the weighted average of the betas of the assets that comprise the portfolio:

$$\beta_P = (0.25)(1.60) + (0.10)(0.50) + (0.75)(1.0) + (-0.20)(0.80) + (0.10)(0) = 1.04$$

e)

$$\overline{r} = r_f + \beta(\overline{R}_M - r_f) = 0.06 + (1.04)(0.16 - 0.06) = 0.164 = 16.4\%$$

6.1)

(1)

$$x_1 \left(\tilde{r}_1 = \alpha_1 + \beta_{11} \tilde{F}_1 + \beta_{12} \tilde{F}_2 + ... + \beta_{1K} \tilde{F}_K + \tilde{\varepsilon}_1 \right)$$
$$x_2 \left(\tilde{r}_2 = \alpha_2 + \beta_{21} \tilde{F}_1 + \beta_{22} \tilde{F}_2 + ... + \beta_{2K} \tilde{F}_K + \tilde{\varepsilon}_2 \right)$$
$$\vdots$$
$$x_N \left(\tilde{r}_N = \alpha_N + \beta_{N1} \tilde{F}_1 + \beta_{N2} \tilde{F}_2 + ... + \beta_{NK} \tilde{F}_K + \tilde{\varepsilon}_N \right)$$

$$\tilde{R}_p = \alpha_p + \beta_{p1} \tilde{F}_1 + \beta_{p2} \tilde{F}_2 + ... + \beta_{pK} \tilde{F}_K + \tilde{\varepsilon}_p$$
$$\tilde{R}_p = x_1 \tilde{r}_1 + x_2 \tilde{r}_2 + ... + x_N \tilde{r}_N$$
$$\alpha_p = x_1 \alpha_1 + x_2 \alpha_2 + ... + x_N \alpha_N$$
$$\beta_{p1} = x_1 \beta_{11} + x_2 \beta_{21} + ... + x_N \beta_{N1}$$
$$\beta_{p2} = x_1 \beta_{12} + x_2 \beta_{22} + ... + x_N \beta_{N2}$$
$$\vdots$$
$$\beta_{pK} = x_1 \beta_{1K} + x_2 \beta_{2K} + ... + x_N \beta_{NK}$$
$$\tilde{\varepsilon}_p = x_1 \tilde{\varepsilon}_1 + x_2 \tilde{\varepsilon}_2 + ... + x_N \tilde{\varepsilon}_N$$

(2)

$$x_1 \tilde{r}_1 + ... + x_N \tilde{r}_N = \left(x_1 \alpha_1 + ... + x_N \alpha_N \right) + \left(x_1 \beta_{11} + ... + x_N \beta_{N1} \right) \tilde{F}_1 + ...$$
$$+ \left(x_1 \beta_{1K} + ... + x_N \beta_{NK} \right) \tilde{F}_K + \left(x_1 \tilde{\varepsilon}_1 + ... + x_N \tilde{\varepsilon}_N \right)$$

(3)

$$x_1 \tilde{r}_1 + ... + x_N \tilde{r}_N = \left(x_1 \alpha_1 + ... + x_N \alpha_N \right) + \left(x_1 \frac{\text{cov}(\tilde{r}_1, \tilde{F}_1)}{\text{var}(\tilde{F}_1)} + ... + x_N \frac{\text{cov}(\tilde{r}_N, \tilde{F}_1)}{\text{var}(\tilde{F}_1)} \right) \tilde{F}_1$$
$$+ ... + \left(x_1 \frac{\text{cov}(\tilde{r}_1, \tilde{F}_K)}{\text{var}(\tilde{F}_K)} + ... + x_N \frac{\text{cov}(\tilde{r}_N, \tilde{F}_K)}{\text{var}(\tilde{F}_K)} \right) \tilde{F}_K + \tilde{\varepsilon}_p$$

(4)

$$\text{cov}\left(\tilde{R}_p, \tilde{F}_1 \right) = x_1 \, \text{cov}\left(\tilde{r}_1, \tilde{F}_1 \right) + x_2 \, \text{cov}\left(\tilde{r}_2, \tilde{F}_1 \right) + ... + x_N \, \text{cov}\left(\tilde{r}_N, \tilde{F}_1 \right)$$
$$= \text{cov}\left(x_1 \tilde{r}_1 + ... + x_N \tilde{r}_N, \tilde{F}_1 \right)$$
$$= \text{cov}\left(x_1 \tilde{r}_1, \tilde{F}_1 \right) + ... + \text{cov}\left(x_N \tilde{r}_N, \tilde{F}_1 \right)$$
$$= x_1 \, \text{cov}\left(\tilde{r}_1, \tilde{F}_1 \right) + ... + x_N \, \text{cov}\left(\tilde{r}_N, \tilde{F}_1 \right)$$

The analogous equation holds for all factors F_j, where $j = 1,...,K$. Therefore, we can write:

$$\widetilde{R}_p = \alpha_p + \frac{\mathrm{cov}(\widetilde{R}_p, \widetilde{F}_1)}{\mathrm{var}(\widetilde{F}_1)}\widetilde{F}_1 + ... + \frac{\mathrm{cov}(\widetilde{R}_p, \widetilde{F}_K)}{\mathrm{var}(\widetilde{F}_K)}\widetilde{F}_K + \widetilde{\varepsilon}_p$$

$$\Rightarrow \beta_{p1} = x_1\beta_{11} + x_2\beta_{21} + ... + x_N\beta_{N1} = \frac{\mathrm{cov}(\widetilde{R}_p, \widetilde{F}_1)}{\mathrm{var}(\widetilde{F}_1)}.$$

$$\vdots$$

$$\Rightarrow \beta_{pK} = x_1\beta_{1K} + x_2\beta_{2K} + ... + x_N\beta_{NK} = \frac{\mathrm{cov}(\widetilde{R}_p, \widetilde{F}_K)}{\mathrm{var}(\widetilde{F}_K)}.$$

6.2)

Nine factors generate nine risk premia plus one implicit risk-free rate that can exactly explain any ten expected returns.

6.3)

$$\sigma_A^2 = 36\,\mathrm{var}(F_1) + 16\,\mathrm{var}(F_2) + \mathrm{var}(\varepsilon_A)$$
$$= 36(0.01) + 16(0.01) + 0.01$$
$$= 0.53$$

$$\sigma_B^2 = 4\,\mathrm{var}(F_1) + 4\,\mathrm{var}(F_2) + \mathrm{var}(\varepsilon_B)$$
$$= 4(0.01) + 4(0.01) + 0.04$$
$$= 0.12$$

$$\sigma_C^2 = 25\,\mathrm{var}(F_1) + 1\,\mathrm{var}(F_2) + \mathrm{var}(\varepsilon_c)$$
$$= 25(0.01) + 1(0.01) + 0.02$$
$$= 0.28$$

$$\sigma_{AB} = \mathrm{cov}(6F_1 + 4F_2 + \varepsilon_A, 2F_1 + 2F_2 + \varepsilon_B)$$
$$= \mathrm{cov}(6F_1, 2F_1) + \mathrm{cov}(4F_2, 2F_2)$$
$$= 12\,\mathrm{var}(F_1) + 8\,\mathrm{var}(F_2)$$
$$= 12(0.01) + 8(0.01)$$
$$= 0.20$$

$$\sigma_{BC} = \mathrm{cov}(2F_1, 5F_1) + \mathrm{cov}(2F_2, -1F_2)$$
$$= 10\,\mathrm{var}(F_1) - 2\,\mathrm{var}(F_2)$$
$$= 10(0.01) - 2(0.01)$$
$$= 0.08$$

$$\sigma_{AC} = \mathrm{cov}(6F_1, 5F_1) + \mathrm{cov}(4F_2, -1F_2)$$
$$= 30(0.01) - 4(0.01)$$
$$= 0.26$$

$$\rho_{AB} = \frac{\sigma_{AB}}{\sigma_A \sigma_B} = \frac{0.20}{\sqrt{(0.53)(0.12)}} = 0.793$$

$$\rho_{BC} = \frac{\sigma_{BC}}{\sigma_B \sigma_C} = \frac{0.08}{\sqrt{(0.28)(0.12)}} = 0.436$$

$$\rho_{AC} = \frac{\sigma_{AC}}{\sigma_A \sigma_C} = \frac{0.26}{\sqrt{(0.53)(0.28)}} = 0.675$$

6.4)

$$\bar{r}_A = .13 + 6\bar{F}_1 + 4\bar{F}_2 + \bar{\varepsilon}_A = .13 + 6(0) + 4(0) + 0 = 0.13 = 13.0\%$$
$$\bar{r}_B = .15 + 2\bar{F}_1 + 2\bar{F}_2 + \bar{\varepsilon}_B = .15 + 2(0) + 2(0) + 0 = 0.15 = 15.0\%$$
$$\bar{r}_C = .07 + 5\bar{F}_1 - 1\bar{F}_2 + \bar{\varepsilon}_C = .07 + 5(0) - 1(0) + 0 = 0.07 = 7.0\%$$

6.5)

$$(1) R_p = 2r_A - 2r_B + 1r_C$$
$$= 2(0.13 + 6F_1 + 4F_2 + \varepsilon_A) - 2(0.15 + 2F_1 + 2F_2 + \varepsilon_B) + .07 + 5F_1 - F_2 + \varepsilon_C$$
$$R_p = .03 + 13F_1 + 3F_2 + \varepsilon_p$$
$$E(R_p) = .03 = 3.0\%$$

$$(2) R_p = \frac{20}{7}r_A - \frac{20}{7}r_B + \frac{10}{7}r_C - \frac{3}{7}r_C$$
$$= \frac{20}{7}r_A - \frac{20}{7}r_B + r_C$$
$$= \frac{20}{7}(0.13 + 6F_1 + 4F_2 + \varepsilon_A) - \frac{20}{7}(0.15 + 2F_1 + 2F_2 + \varepsilon_B) + (.07 + 5F_1 - F_2 + \varepsilon_C)$$
$$= 0.371 + \frac{120}{7}F_1 + \frac{80}{7}F_2 - 0.429 - \frac{40}{7}F_1 - \frac{40}{7}F_2 + 0.07 + 5F_1 - F_2 + \varepsilon_p$$
$$= .0129 + \frac{115}{7}F_1 + \frac{33}{7}F_2 + \varepsilon_p$$
$$E(R_p) = .0129 = 1.29\%$$

6.6)

$$6x_A + 2x_B + 5(1 - x_A - x_B) = 1$$
$$4x_A + 2x_B - 1(1 - x_A - x_B) = 0$$
$$x_A - 3x_B = -4$$
$$5x_A + 3x_B = 1$$
$$6x_A = -3$$

Portfolio 1: $x_A = -\dfrac{1}{2}$

$$x_B = \dfrac{7}{6}$$

$$x_C = \dfrac{1}{3}$$

$$6x_A + 2x_B + 5(1 - x_A - x_B) = 0$$
$$4x_A + 2x_B - 1(1 - x_A - x_B) = 1$$
$$x_A - 3x_B = -5$$
$$5x_A + 3x_B = 2$$
$$6x_A = -3$$

Portfolio 2: $x_A = -\dfrac{1}{2}$

$$x_B = \dfrac{3}{2}$$

$$x_C = 0$$

$$\overline{R}_{p1} = -\frac{1}{2}(0.13) + \frac{7}{6}(0.15) + \frac{1}{3}(0.07) = .1333 = 13.33\%$$

$$\overline{R}_{p2} = -\frac{1}{2}(0.13) + \frac{3}{2}(0.15) = 0.16 = 16.0\%$$

$$6x_A + 2x_B + 5 - 5x_A - 5x_B = 0$$

$$4x_A + 2x_B - 1 + x_A + x_B = 0$$
$$x_A - 3x_B = -5$$
$$5x_A + 3x_B = 1$$
$$6x_A = -4$$

$$x_A = -\dfrac{2}{3}$$

$$x_B = \dfrac{13}{9}$$

$$x_C = \dfrac{2}{9}$$

$$\bar{R}_p = -\frac{2}{3}(0.13) + \frac{13}{9}(0.15) + \frac{2}{9}(0.07) = 0.1456 = 14.56\%$$
$$\lambda_1 = 0.1333 - 0.1456 = -0.0123 = -1.23\%$$
$$\lambda_2 = .16 - .1456 = .0144 = 1.44\%$$

6.7)

$$\tilde{r}_{uni} = 0.11 + 2\tilde{F} + \tilde{\varepsilon}_{uni}$$
$$\tilde{r}_{due} = 0.17 + 5\tilde{F} + \tilde{\varepsilon}_{due}$$

$$2x + 5(1 - x) = -3$$
$$-3x + 5 = -3$$
$$-3x = -8$$
$$x = \frac{8}{3}$$
$$x_{uni} = \frac{8}{3}, \quad x_{due} = -\frac{5}{3}$$
$$\bar{R}_p = \frac{8}{3}(0.11) - \frac{5}{3}(0.17) = 0.0100 = 1.00\%$$

6.8)

You could design a portfolio of the forty largest stocks that mimics the factor betas of the S&P 500, and thus "tracks" its movements. Due to transaction costs, this might be preferred to investing in all 500 stocks.

6.9)

$$\tilde{r}_i = \alpha_i + \beta_i \tilde{R}_M + \tilde{\varepsilon}_i$$
$$\bar{r}_i = \alpha_i + \beta_i \bar{R}_M$$

If the CAPM holds, then:

$$\bar{r}_i = r_f + \beta_i (\bar{R}_M - r_f) = r_f - \beta_i r_f + \beta_i \bar{R}_M$$

Thus:

$$\alpha_i = r_f - \beta_i r_f = (1 - \beta_i) r_f$$

6.10)

Since there are only two types of stock with differing firm-specific variance, the same amount x is invested in each of the first ten stocks and the same amount y is invested in each of the second ten stocks. In order for the weights to add to one:

$$y = 1/10 - x$$

Since the variances of the stocks are firm specific, there are no covariance terms. Thus, we wish to minimize:

$$\text{var}(\widetilde{R}_p) = (1/10)[x^2(0.10)(10) + (0.1\text{-}x)^2(0.05)(10)]$$

By setting the derivative of the portfolio's firm-specific variance to zero with respect to x, we can solve for the weight that minimizes firm-specific variance:

$$\frac{\partial\,\text{var}(\widetilde{R}_p)}{\partial x} = 2x(0.10)(10) - (0.2)(0.05)(10) + 2x(0.05)(10) = 0$$

$$3x = 0.1$$

So, invest $\dfrac{1}{30}$ in each of the first ten securities (with firm-specific variance $= 0.10$), and $\dfrac{2}{30}$ or $\dfrac{1}{15}$ in each of the second ten securities.

The variance and standard deviation of the portfolio are:

$$\text{var}(R_p) = (1/30)^2(0.10)(10) + (2/30)^2(0.05)(10)$$

$$= 0.00333$$

$$\sigma(R_p) = \sqrt{0.00333} = 0.0577$$

6.11)

Let $x_1 =$ the weight for Security 1, $x_2 =$ the weight for Security 2 and $x_3 = 1 - x_1 - x_2 =$ the weight for Security 3. Then, the first pure factor portfolio is found by solving the following two equations:

$$2x_1 + 3x_2 + 3(1 - x_1 - x_2) = 1$$

$$2x_1 + x_2 + 0(1 - x_1 - x_2) = 0$$

The first equation simplifies to $x_1 = 2$, which can be substituted into the second equation. Therefore, the weights are: $x_1 = 2$, $x_2 = -4$ and $x_3 = 3$. The expected return for this portfolio is:

$$2(0.06) - 4(0.05) + 3(0.04) = 0.04$$

The factor equation is:

$$\widetilde{R}_{p1} = .04 + \widetilde{F}_1$$

The second pure factor portfolio is found by solving the following two equations:

$$2x_1 + 3x_2 + 3(1 - x_1 - x_2) = 0$$

$$2x_1 + x_2 + 0(1 - x_1 - x_2) = 1$$

The first equation simplifies to $x_1 = 3$, which can be substituted into the second equation. Therefore, the weights are: $x_1 = 3$, $x_2 = -5$ and $x_3 = 3$. The expected return for this portfolio is:

$$3(0.06) - 5(0.05) + 3(0.04) = 0.05$$

The factor equation is:

$$\widetilde{R}_{p2} = .05 + \widetilde{F}_2$$

The risk premiums of the two pure factor portfolios are λ_1 and λ_2, respectively. In order to determine the values of λ_1 and λ_2, solve for a risk free portfolio by solving the following equations:

$$2x_1 + 3x_2 + 3(1 - x_1 - x_2) = 0$$

$$2x_1 + x_2 + 0(1 - x_1 - x_2) = 0$$

The solution to these equations is: $x_1 = 3$, $x_2 = -6$ and $x_3 = 4$. The expected return for this risk free portfolio is:

$$(3)(0.06) + (-6)(0.05) + (4)(0.04) = 0.04$$

Therefore, λ_1 is 0 (the expected return for the first pure factor portfolio (0.04) minus the risk free rate) and λ_2 is 0.01 (the expected return for the second pure factor portfolio (0.05) minus the risk free rate.

Note that the risk free rate and the risk premiums can also be determined by first solving for r_f in the APT equation for any one of the three assets. For example, using the APT equation for Security 1:

$$\bar{r}_i = r_f + \beta_1 \lambda_1 + \beta_2 \lambda_2$$
$$0.06 = r_f + 2(0.04 - r_f) + 2(0.05 - r_f)$$

Solving this equation: $r_f = 0.04$, $\lambda_1 = 0$, $\lambda_2 = 0.01$

6.12)

The pure factor portfolio from Exercise 6.11 has the factor equation:

$$\tilde{R}_{p1} = .04 + 1\tilde{F}_1 + 0\tilde{F}_2$$

Security 4 has the factor equation:

$$\tilde{R}_4 = .08 + 1\tilde{F}_1 + 0\tilde{F}_2$$

Therefore, an arbitrage opportunity does exist. The arbitrage opportunity requires that we purchase the high expected return stock (i.e., Security 4) and short its tracking portfolio. This is achieved by shorting the pure factor portfolio constructed from the three securities in Exercise 6.11. For every dollar of Security 4 purchased, short \$2 of Security 1, buy \$4 of Security 2 and short \$3 of Security 3. Such a position has no factor risk, costs nothing today, and generates (\$0.08 − \$0.04) = \$0.04 in the future for every dollar of Security 4 purchased. This is an arbitrage that can be scaled to any degree.

6.13)

[Note to instructor: In the first printing of the second edition, Exercise 6.13 refers to the 'solid and dotted *red* lines in Exhibit 6.7.' The lines in Exhibit 6.7 in the text are actually *blue*. The incorrect wording of Exercise 6.13 will be corrected in the second printing.]

Example 6.10 indicates that the solid line representing Security 2 corresponds to the equation:

$$.08 = .05 + .02\lambda_1 + .01\lambda_2$$

The dotted line representing Security 3 corresponds to the equation:

$.15 = .05 + .04\lambda_1 + .04\lambda_2$

The simultaneous solution to these two equations is shown in Example 6.9 as:

$\lambda_1 = 0.5$ and $\lambda_2 = 2$

Hence, the coordinates of the intersection of the solid and dotted lines are (0.5,2).

CHAPTER 7
PRICING DERIVATIVES

7.1)

Working through the asset value tree, we can compute the risk neutral probabilities at each node. The risk neutral probabilities π for each node satisfy:

$$\pi_s = \frac{1 + r_f - d}{u - d}$$

Step 1: The payoffs at node u are:

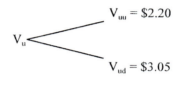

Using the formula we get, at node u :

$$\pi_u = \frac{(1+.04) - \$1.05/\$1.10}{[\$1.20 - \$1.05]/\$1.10} = 0.6267$$

Using these risk neutral probabilities, we get the time 1 expected payoff of the derivative (V) at time 2, if we are at node u:

$$E_u[V_2] = .6267 \times \$2.20 + (1 - .6267) \times \$3.05 = \$2.5173$$

The present value of those cash flows at time 1 is:

$$PV_1(E_u[V_2]) = \frac{\$2.5173}{1 + .04} = \$2.4205$$

Step 2: The payoffs at node d are:

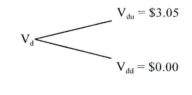

We get at node d:

$$\pi_d = \frac{(1+.04) - \$.90/\$.95}{[\$1.05 - \$.90]/\$.95} = 0.5867$$

Using these risk neutral probabilities, we get the time 1 expected payoff of D at time 2, if we are at node d:

$$E_d[V_2] = .5867 \times \$3.05 + (1 - .5867) \times \$0 = \$1.7894$$

The present value of those cash flows at time 1 is:

$$PV_1(E_d[V_2]) = \frac{\$1.7894}{1+.04} = \$1.7206$$

Step 3: In this step, the payoffs of the derivative include the stated payoff in the state plus the PV of the expected payoffs in period 2 if we end up in this state.

$S_u = \$1.10$

$S_0 = \$1$

$S_d = \$0.95$

$V_u = \$.10 + \$2.42$

V_0

$V_d = \$.90 + \$1.72$

Hence, we get at node 0:

$$\pi_0 = \frac{(1+.04) - .95}{1.1 - .95} = 0.60$$

Using these risk neutral probabilities, we get the time 0 expected payoff at time 1:

$$E_0[V_1] = .60 \times (\$0.10 + \$2.42) + (1 - .60) \times (\$0.90 + \$1.72) = \$2.56$$

The present value of those cash flows at time 1 is:

$$PV_0(E_0[V_1]) = \frac{\$2.56}{1+.04} = \$2.46$$

7.2)

The payoff structures of the underlying stock and the bond are as follows:

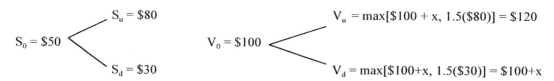

$S_u = \$80$

$S_0 = \$50$

$S_d = \$30$

$V_u = \max[\$100 + x, \ 1.5(\$80)] = \$120$

$V_0 = \$100$

$V_d = \max[\$100+x, \ 1.5(\$30)] = \$100+x$

Since the risk free rate is 15%, x is, at most, \$15, and the convertibility feature is valuable and would be exercised in the up state for a payoff of $(1.5 \times \$80) = \$120$. In this instance, instead of knowing the payoffs of the underlying security and the derivative at the terminal point and solving for the upfront cost of the derivative, we know the cost of the derivative and its payoff in the up state, and have to solve for the payoff in the down state. Form a portfolio of the stock and the riskless asset that has the same up payoff and the same cost as the bond and compute its payoff in the down state. To prevent arbitrage, the bond payoff in the down state has to be equal to the tracking portfolio payoff in the down state. Hence, construct a portfolio of Δ units of the stock and $[\beta(1.15)]$ of face value of the riskfree asset, such that the portfolio has the same payoffs as the bond in the up state and the same cost as the bond. This yields the following system of 2 equations and 2 unknowns:

(i) $\Delta S_u + \beta(1+.15) = V_u$ $\Rightarrow$ $\Delta(\$80) + \beta(1+.15) = \$120$

(ii) $\Delta S_0 + \beta = V_0$ $\Rightarrow$ $\Delta(\$57.50) + \beta(1+.15) = \$115$

Solving for β and Δ yields:

$$\Delta = \frac{\$120 - \$115}{\$80 - \$57.50} = 0.22222$$

$$1.15\beta = \$120 - .22222(\$80) = \$102.222$$

Hence, the payoff of the contract in the down state is:

$$V_d = \Delta S_d + \beta(1.15) = .22222(\$30) + \$102.222 = \$108.89$$

Thus, in equilibrium, the coupon rate of the bond is 8.89%. The corporation saves on coupon payments (8.89% vs. 15%) at the cost of forfeiting participation in the gains if the company does well.

7.3)

To value the bond you can consider the terminal payments independent of the intermediate coupon payment. This is because the company has put ($5/1.04) in a reserve to pay for the coupon, and that reserve is excluded from the underlying asset value. The terminal payoffs of the bond in each state of the world will be the minimum of $105 or the value of the assets in that state of the world.

$r_f = 4\%$ per 6 months

FV=$100, 5% coupon

The risk-neutral probabilities and present value of expected payoffs are computed for node u as:

$$\$120(1.04) = \pi(\$300) + (1 - \pi)(\$110)$$

$$\$124.80 = \$190\pi + \$110$$

$$\pi = .078$$

$$V_u = \frac{(.078)(\$105) + (1 - .078)(\$105)}{1.04} = \$100.962$$

For node d:

$$\$90(1.04) = \pi(\$110) + (1 - \pi)\$50$$

$$\$93.6 = \$60\pi + \$50$$

$$\pi = .727$$

$$V_d = \frac{(.727)(\$105) + (1 - .727)(\$50)}{1.04} = \$86.524$$

For node 0:

$$\$100(1.04) = \$120\pi + \$90(1 - \pi)$$

$$\$104 = \$30\pi + \$90$$

$$\pi = .467$$

$$V_0 = \frac{[(.467)(\$5 + \$100.962) + (1 - .467)(\$5 + \$86.524)]}{1.04} = \$94.487$$

7.4)

This is the same problem as Exercise 7.3, but now the firm can call the bond for \$105. Since \$105 is less than \$105.962, the firm should call the bond in the up state at time 1. Thus, since $V_d = \$91.524$, then:

$$V_0 = \frac{[(.467)(\$105) + (1 - .467)(\$91.524)]}{1.04} = \$94.055$$

7.5)

In order to determine V_0, we proceed backwards through the tree. The risk free rate is $r_f = 10\%$ throughout.

Step 1: The payoffs at node uu are:

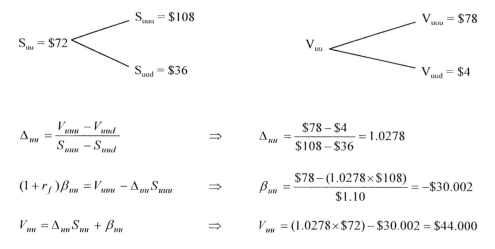

$$\Delta_{uu} = \frac{V_{uuu} - V_{uud}}{S_{uuu} - S_{uud}} \qquad \Rightarrow \qquad \Delta_{uu} = \frac{\$78 - \$4}{\$108 - \$36} = 1.0278$$

$$(1 + r_f)\beta_{uu} = V_{uuu} - \Delta_{uu}S_{uuu} \qquad \Rightarrow \qquad \beta_{uu} = \frac{\$78 - (1.0278 \times \$108)}{\$1.10} = -\$30.002$$

$$V_{uu} = \Delta_{uu}S_{uu} + \beta_{uu} \qquad \Rightarrow \qquad V_{uu} = (1.0278 \times \$72) - \$30.002 = \$44.000$$

Step 2: The payoffs at node *ud* are:

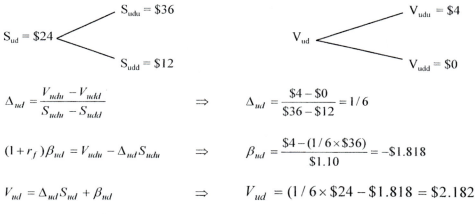

$$\Delta_{ud} = \frac{V_{udu} - V_{udd}}{S_{udu} - S_{udd}} \qquad \Rightarrow \qquad \Delta_{ud} = \frac{\$4 - \$0}{\$36 - \$12} = 1/6$$

$$(1 + r_f)\beta_{ud} = V_{udu} - \Delta_{ud}S_{udu} \qquad \Rightarrow \qquad \beta_{ud} = \frac{\$4 - (1/6 \times \$36)}{\$1.10} = -\$1.818$$

$$V_{ud} = \Delta_{ud}S_{ud} + \beta_{ud} \qquad \Rightarrow \qquad V_{ud} = (1/6 \times \$24 - \$1.818 = \$2.182$$

Step 3: The payoffs at node *dd* are:

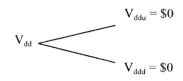

Since the derivative's future payoffs are zero in this case, its value is zero: $V_{dd} = \$0$

Step 4: The payoffs at node *u* are:

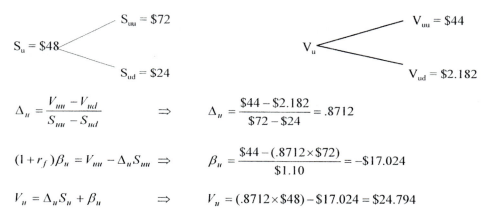

$$\Delta_u = \frac{V_{uu} - V_{ud}}{S_{uu} - S_{ud}} \qquad \Rightarrow \qquad \Delta_u = \frac{\$44 - \$2.182}{\$72 - \$24} = .8712$$

$$(1 + r_f)\beta_u = V_{uu} - \Delta_u S_{uu} \qquad \Rightarrow \qquad \beta_u = \frac{\$44 - (.8712 \times \$72)}{\$1.10} = -\$17.024$$

$$V_u = \Delta_u S_u + \beta_u \qquad \Rightarrow \qquad V_u = (.8712 \times \$48) - \$17.024 = \$24.794$$

Step 5: The payoffs at node d are:

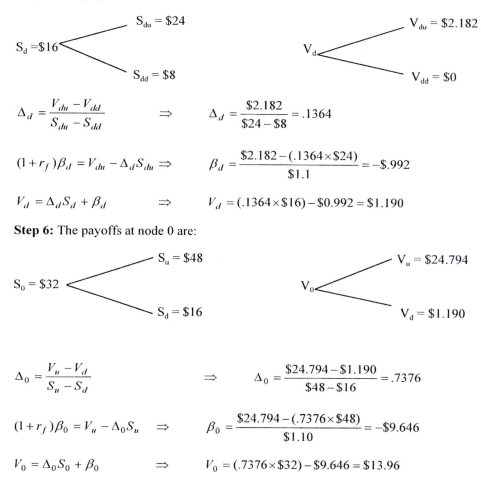

$$\Delta_d = \frac{V_{du} - V_{dd}}{S_{du} - S_{dd}} \quad\Rightarrow\quad \Delta_d = \frac{\$2.182}{\$24 - \$8} = .1364$$

$$(1 + r_f)\beta_d = V_{du} - \Delta_d S_{du} \quad\Rightarrow\quad \beta_d = \frac{\$2.182 - (.1364 \times \$24)}{\$1.1} = -\$.992$$

$$V_d = \Delta_d S_d + \beta_d \quad\Rightarrow\quad V_d = (.1364 \times \$16) - \$0.992 = \$1.190$$

Step 6: The payoffs at node 0 are:

$$\Delta_0 = \frac{V_u - V_d}{S_u - S_d} \quad\Rightarrow\quad \Delta_0 = \frac{\$24.794 - \$1.190}{\$48 - \$16} = .7376$$

$$(1 + r_f)\beta_0 = V_u - \Delta_0 S_u \quad\Rightarrow\quad \beta_0 = \frac{\$24.794 - (.7376 \times \$48)}{\$1.10} = -\$9.646$$

$$V_0 = \Delta_0 S_0 + \beta_0 \quad\Rightarrow\quad V_0 = (.7376 \times \$32) - \$9.646 = \$13.96$$

7.6)

a)

	Cost Today	CF in future
Forward	$10.75	$S_1 - \$150$
Tracking	$140 – ($150)(98/100) = –$7	$S_1 - \$150$

Since the price of the forward ($10.75) is not the same as the price of the tracking portfolio (–$7), you should buy the tracking portfolio (by buying IBM stock and financing the purchase with bond borrowings) and sell the forward contract on IBM at $10.75. This strategy generates $17.75 in arbitrage profits.

b)

The value of the tracking portfolio is now:

$160 – ($150)(99/100) = $11.50

Assuming no arbitrage, the fair market value of the forward contract is $11.50, an increase of $18.50 over its previous fair market value of –$7.

7.7)

a)

		Cash flow out today	Cash flow in the future
Sony	Forward	$0	S_1–$100
	Tracking	–$90+$93=$3	S_1–$100
	Tracking–Forward	$3	$0

		Cash flow out today	Cash flow in the future
Disney	Forward	$0.00	S_1–$40
	Tracking	–$35+($40)(93/100)	S_1–$40
	Tracking–Forward	$2.20	$0.00

Since both $3.00 and $2.20 are greater than zero, there are arbitrage opportunities (short forward, long tracking portfolio) for Sony, for Disney, or for both.

b)

	Cash flow out today	Cash flow in the future
Forward on portfolio	$V_{portfolio}$	S–$70
½ Sony forward	V_{Sony}	$\frac{1}{2}S_{Sony}$–$50
½ Disney forward	V_{Disney}	$\frac{1}{2}S_{Disney}$–$20
Tracking portfolio	(–1/2)×90–(1/2×35)+ 70×93/100=$2.60	$\frac{1}{2}S_{Sony}$+$\frac{1}{2}S_{Disney}$–$70

c)

	Cash flow out today	Cash flow in the future
Forward on portfolio	$V_{portfolio}$	$S-\$70$
½ Sony forward	V_{Sony}	$\frac{1}{2}S_{Sony}-\$50$
½ Disney forward	V_{Disney}	$\frac{1}{2}S_{Disney}-\$20$
Tracking portfolio	$(-1/2)\times90-(1/2\times35)+$ $70\times93/100=\$2.60$	$\frac{1}{2}S_{Sony}+\frac{1}{2}S_{Disney}-\$70$

Since they have the same tracking portfolios, the prices $V_{portfolio}$ and $V_{Sony}+V_{Disney}$ should be the same. Otherwise, there is arbitrage.

d)

Yes, for no arbitrage to hold, the same cash flows must have the same price.

7.8)

	Eurodollar	Euro £
9-month interest rate	$274/360 \times 9\%$	$274/360 \times 11\%$
(Unannualized)	$= 6.85\%$	$= 8.37\%$

$$\text{forward rate} = \frac{1+0.0685}{1+0.0837}\times1.58 = 1.5578\$/£$$

7.9)

From Equation 7.5, which uses risk-neutral probabilities, π is determined as follows:

$$1 = 1.15\pi + (0.9)(1-\pi) \Rightarrow \pi = .40$$
$$V = \frac{(0.40)(\$25)+(0.60)(-\$5)}{1.10} = \$6.36$$

(The actual probabilities are irrelevant for determining the option's price.)

7.10)

The derivative pays $20 if two up moves occur, $10 if one up move occurs and $0 otherwise. The risk-neutral probability attached to each up state is:

$$\pi = \frac{1+r_f-d}{u-d} = \frac{1.06-.8}{1.2-.8} = 0.65$$

After one up move, the derivative is worth:

$$V_u = \frac{(.65)(\$20) + (1 - .65)(\$10)}{1.06} = \frac{\$16.50}{1.06}$$

After one down move, the derivative is worth

$$V_d = \frac{(.65)(\$10) + (1 - .65)(\$0)}{1.06} = \frac{\$6.50}{1.06}$$

Therefore, at the initial date, the derivative is worth:

$$V_0 = \frac{(.65)(\$16.50/1.06) + (1 - .65)(\$6.50/1.06)}{1.06} = \frac{\$13.00}{1.06^2} = \$11.57$$

7.11)

T = number of years to expiration = 0.5

N = number of binomial periods = 8

T/N = the number of years per binomial period = 0.5/8 = 0.0625

$$u = e^{\sigma\sqrt{T/N}} = e^{0.3\sqrt{0.0625}} = 1.0779$$
$$d = 1/u = 0.9277$$

7.12)

The risk neutral probabilities satisfy:

$50 = [\$80 \pi + \$30 (1 - \pi)]/1.15$

The solution is: $\pi = 0.55$

The zero-cost forward price is: F = ($80 × 0.55) + [$30 × (1 − 0.55)] = $57.50

Note that the forward price can also be obtained from Result 7.2:

$$F_0 = S_0(1 + r_f)^T = \$50(1.15)^1 = \$57.50$$

7.13)

a)

After two periods, the underlying security (i.e., ABC stock) and the Tootsie Square have the following values:

	ABC Stock	Tootsie Square
Two up moves	$1 × (1.10²)	$1 × (1.10⁴)
One up move, one down move	$1 × (1.10 × 0.95)	$1 × (1.10 × 0.95)²
Two down moves	$1 × (.95²)	$1 × (.95⁴)

46

The risk neutral probability for an up move is:

$$\pi = \frac{1 + r_f - d}{u - d} = \frac{1.05 - .95}{1.10 - .95} = 2/3$$

Thus, after one up move, the Tootsie Square is worth:

$$V_u = \frac{(2/3)(\$1 \times 1.10^4) + (1/3)[(\$1) \times (1.10 \times 0.95)^2]}{1.05} = \$1.276$$

After one down move, the Tootsie Square is worth:

$$V_u = \frac{(2/3)[(\$1) \times (1.10 \times 0.95)^2] + (1/3)(\$1 \times 0.95^4)}{1.05} = \$0.952$$

Therefore, at the initial date, the Tootsie Square is worth:

$$V_0 = \frac{(2/3)(\$1.276) + (1/3)(\$0.952)}{1.05} = \$1.112$$

b)

To find the tracking portfolio, let Δ represent the number of shares of ABC stock and let B represent the number of dollars invested in the risk-free security. The equations corresponding to the up node and the down node, respectively, are:

$$\Delta S_u + B(1 + r_f) = V_u$$
$$\Delta S_d + B(1 + r_f) = V_d$$

For the values in this exercise, the two equations are:

$$\Delta(1.10) + B(1.05) = (1.10)^2 = 1.21$$
$$\Delta(0.95) + B(1.05) = (0.95)^2 = 0.9025$$

The simultaneous solution to these equations is: $\Delta = 2.05$ and $B = -0.9952$ so that the tracking portfolio has 2.05 shares of ABC stock.

8.1)

American call: K = $30, S = $35

Strategy (1): exercise now, deposit proceeds in a bank account:

at t = 1: $5 $(1+ r_f)$

Strategy (2):	hold option	short stock
	max $(S_1-\$30, 0)$	$35 (1+ r_f) - S_1$

If $S_1 > \$30 \Rightarrow CF = S_1 - \$30 + \$35(1 + r_f) - S_1$

$$= \$35(1 + r_f) - \$30$$
$$= \$30(1 + r_f - 1) + \$5(1 + r_f)$$
$$= \$30 r_f + \$5(1 + r_f)$$

If $S_1 < \$30 \Rightarrow CF = 0 + \$35(1 + r_f) - S_1$

$$= \$5(1 + r_f) + \$30(1 + r_f) - S_1$$

In either case, strategy 2 produces the greater cash flow.

8.2)

Put-call parity: $c_0 = S_0 - PV(K) + p_0$

Black-Scholes formula for European calls:

$$c_0 = S_0 \cdot N\left\{\frac{\ln[S_0/PV(K)]}{\sigma\sqrt{T}} + \frac{\sigma\sqrt{T}}{2}\right\} - PV(K) \cdot N\left\{\frac{\ln[S_0/PV(K)]}{\sigma\sqrt{T}} - \frac{\sigma\sqrt{T}}{2}\right\}$$

Set the put-call parity formula equal to the Black-Scholes formula:

$$S_0 - PV(K) + p_0 =$$

$$S_0 \cdot N\left\{\frac{\ln[S_0/PV(K)]}{\sigma\sqrt{T}} + \frac{\sigma\sqrt{T}}{2}\right\} - PV(K) \cdot N\left\{\frac{\ln[S_0/PV(K)]}{\sigma\sqrt{T}} - \frac{\sigma\sqrt{T}}{2}\right\}$$

Solve for p_0:

$$p_0 = S_0 \cdot N\left\{\frac{\ln[S_0/PV(K)]}{\sigma\sqrt{T}} + \frac{\sigma\sqrt{T}}{2}\right\} - PV(K) \cdot N\left\{\frac{\ln[S_0/PV(K)]}{\sigma\sqrt{T}} - \frac{\sigma\sqrt{T}}{2}\right\} - S_0 + PV(K)$$

$$p_0 = S_0 \cdot [N(d_1) - 1] + PV(K)[1 - N(d_1 - \sigma\sqrt{T})]$$

where :

$$d_1 = \frac{\ln[S_0/PV(K)]}{\sigma\sqrt{T}} + \frac{\sigma\sqrt{T}}{2}$$

8.3)

$\sigma = 0.25$, $S_0 = \$60$, $K = \$65$, $c_0 = \$10$, $PV(K) = \$56$

$$c_0 = \$60 \cdot N\left[\frac{\ln\left(\$60/\$56\right)}{0.25\sqrt{1}} + \frac{0.25\sqrt{1}}{2}\right] - \$56N\left[\frac{\ln\left(\$60/\$56\right)}{0.25\sqrt{1}} - \frac{0.25\sqrt{1}}{2}\right]$$

$$= \$60N(0.401) - \$56N(0.151) = \$60(0.6558) - \$56(.5600) = \$7.9880$$

The call selling at $10 is overpriced. It is worth only $7.99. To take advantage of the arbitrage opportunity, sell the call and buy the tracking portfolio. The tracking portfolio requires a long position of $N(d_1) = 0.6558$ shares of the stock and borrowing at the risk-free rate the amount:

$PV(K) \times N(d_1 - \sigma\sqrt{T}) = \$56\ (0.5600) = \$31.36$

If the stock price goes up to $62, then both $N(d_1)$ and $N(d_1 - \sigma\sqrt{T})$ will change and the position in the stock and the amount of borrowing have to be adjusted. At a stock price of $62:

$N(d_1) = N(0.532) = 0.7026$

$N(d_1 - \sigma\sqrt{T}) = N(.282) = 0.6110$

The larger $N(d_1)$ indicates that there is a larger position in the stock. The larger $N(d_1 - \sigma\sqrt{T})$ indicates more risk-free borrowing.

8.4)

[Note: In the first printing of the second edition, the *Hint* at the end of Exercise 8.4 identifies $N'(d_1)$ incorrectly. It should read as follows:

$$N'(d_1) = \frac{1}{\sqrt{2\pi}} e^{-.5d_1^2}]$$

$$c_0 = S_0 \cdot N\left\{\frac{\ln[S_0/PV(K)]}{\sigma\sqrt{T}} + \frac{\sigma\sqrt{T}}{2}\right\} - PV(K) \cdot N\left\{\frac{\ln[S_0/PV(K)]}{\sigma\sqrt{T}} - \frac{\sigma\sqrt{T}}{2}\right\}$$

$$\frac{\partial c_0}{\partial S_0} = N(d_1) + S_0 N'(d_1) - PV(K)N'(d_1 - \sigma\sqrt{T})$$

$$= N(d_1) + S_0 \frac{1}{\sqrt{2\pi}} e^{-.5d_1^2} - PV(K)\frac{1}{\sqrt{2\pi}} e^{-.5(d_1 - \sigma\sqrt{T})^2}$$

$$= N(d_1) + \frac{S_0}{\sqrt{2\pi}} e^{-.5d_1^2} - \frac{PV(K)}{\sqrt{2\pi}} e^{-.5d_1^2 + d_1\sigma\sqrt{T} - .5\sigma^2T}$$

$$= N(d_1) + \frac{S_0}{\sqrt{2\pi}} e^{-.5d_1^2} \cdot \left(\frac{1}{S_0\sigma\sqrt{T}}\right) - \frac{PV(K)}{\sqrt{2\pi}} e^{-.5d_1^2} e^{d_1\sigma\sqrt{T}} e^{-.5\sigma^2T} \cdot \left(\frac{1}{S_0\sigma\sqrt{T}}\right)$$

$$= N(d_1) + \frac{S_0}{\sqrt{2\pi}} e^{-.5d_1^2} \cdot \frac{1}{S_0\sigma\sqrt{T}} - \frac{PV(K)}{\sqrt{2\pi}} e^{-.5d_1^2} e^{\left\{\frac{\ln(S_0/PV(K))}{\sigma\sqrt{T}} + \frac{\sigma\sqrt{T}}{2}\right\}\sigma\sqrt{T}} e^{-.5\sigma^2T} \cdot \left(\frac{1}{S_0\sigma\sqrt{T}}\right)$$

$$= N(d_1) + \frac{1}{\sqrt{2\pi}} e^{-.5d_1^2} \cdot \left(\frac{1}{\sigma\sqrt{T}}\right) - \frac{PV(K)}{\sqrt{2\pi}} e^{-.5d_1^2} e^{\ln(S_0/PV(K))} e^{.5\sigma^2T} e^{-.5\sigma^2T} \left(\frac{1}{S_0\sigma\sqrt{T}}\right)$$

$$= N(d_1) + \frac{1}{\sqrt{2\pi}} e^{-.5d_1^2} \cdot \left(\frac{1}{\sigma\sqrt{T}} \right) - \frac{PV(K)}{\sqrt{2\pi}} e^{-.5d_1^2} \frac{S_0}{PV(K)} \frac{1}{S_0\sigma\sqrt{T}}$$

$$= N(d_1) + 0$$

$$\therefore \frac{\partial c_0}{\partial S_0} = N(d_1) > 0$$

8.5)

$$c_0 = S_0 \cdot N\left\{ \frac{\ln[S_0/PV(K)]}{\sigma\sqrt{T}} + \frac{\sigma\sqrt{T}}{2} \right\} - PV(K) \cdot N\left\{ \frac{\ln[S_0/PV(K)]}{\sigma\sqrt{T}} - \frac{\sigma\sqrt{T}}{2} \right\}$$

$$\frac{\partial c_0}{\partial \sigma} = S_0 N'(d_1)\left\{ \frac{-\ln[S_0/PV(K)]}{\sigma^2\sqrt{T}} + \frac{\sqrt{T}}{2} \right\}$$

$$- PV(K) \cdot N'\left(d_1 - \sigma\sqrt{T}\right)\left\{ \frac{-\ln[S_0/PV(K)]}{\sigma^2\sqrt{T}} - \frac{\sqrt{T}}{2} \right\}$$

$$= S_0 N'(d_1)\left\{ \frac{-\ln[S_0/PV(K)]}{\sigma^2\sqrt{T}} + \frac{\sqrt{T}}{2} \right\}$$

$$- \frac{PV(K)}{\sqrt{2\pi}} e^{-.5d_1^2} \frac{S_0}{PV(K)} \left\{ \frac{-\ln[S_0/PV(K)]}{\sigma^2\sqrt{T}} - \frac{\sqrt{T}}{2} \right\}$$

$$= S_0 N'(d_1)\left\{ \frac{-\ln[S_0/PV(K)]}{\sigma^2\sqrt{T}} \right\} + S_0 N'(d_1)\frac{\sqrt{T}}{2}$$

$$- S_0 N'(d_1)\left\{ \frac{-\ln[S_0/PV(K)]}{\sigma^2\sqrt{T}} \right\} + S_0 N'(d_1)\frac{\sqrt{T}}{2}$$

$$= S_0 N'(d_1)\sqrt{T} > 0$$

8.6)

If $PV(K) = \dfrac{K}{(1+r_f)^T}$ then:

$$c_0 = S_0 N(d_1) - \frac{K}{(1+r_f)^T} N\left(d_1 - \sigma\sqrt{T}\right)$$

$$\frac{\partial c_0}{\partial r_f} = \frac{\partial d_1}{\partial r_f} S_0 N'(d_1) - \frac{\partial PV(K)}{\partial r_f} N\left(d_1 - \sigma\sqrt{T}\right) - \frac{\partial d_1}{\partial r_f} PV(K)N'(d_1 - \sigma\sqrt{T})$$

$$\frac{\partial c_0}{\partial r_f} = \frac{T}{1+r_f} \frac{K}{(1+r_f)^T} N\left(d_1 - \sigma\sqrt{T}\right) + \frac{\partial d_1}{\partial r_f}[S_0 N'(d_1) - PV(K)N'(d_1 - \sigma\sqrt{T})]$$

Since $PV(K) = \dfrac{K}{\left(1 + r_f\right)^T}$ and the expression in brackets is zero, as shown in Exercise 8.4, then:

$$\frac{\partial c_0}{\partial r_f} = \frac{T}{1 + r_f} PV(K)N\left(d_1 - \sigma\sqrt{T}\right)$$

8.7)

Buy the call, sell the stock short, and invest $[PV(K) + PV(div)]$ in the risk free asset. Since $c_0 < [S_0 - PV(K) - PV(div)]$, the initial cash flow is positive. Furthermore, the payoffs at maturity are either positive or zero, as indicated in the following table:

	$S_T < K$	$K < S_T$
$+ c_0$	\$0	$S_T - K$
$- S_0$	$- S_T$	$- S_T$
$+PV(K)$	$+ K$	$+ K$
Total payoffs	$K - S_T$	\$0

(Note that the dividends will be paid prior to the maturity of the option.)

8.8)

The position under consideration can be represented as: $2C(\text{with } K = 30) - P(\text{with } K = 30)$. This position can be decomposed as: $C + [C - P]$. So the sensitivity to stock price changes of this option portfolio is equal to the sensitivity of one call plus the sensitivity of a combination long one call and short one put. The second component of this portfolio (i.e., the combination long one call and short one put) has a sensitivity to stock price changes equal to 1, so that; as stock price changes, the payoff of this position at expiration changes by \$1 for every \$1 change in stock price. This result is derived from the put-call parity equation: $c_0 - p_0 = S_0 - PV(K)$. The put-call parity equation indicates that you can track a combination long one call and short one put by purchasing one share of stock and borrowing the PV of the exercise price. Thus, the position in AT&T stock which shows the same sensitivity to AT&T stock price changes as the portfolio comprised of a long position in two calls and a short position in one put is:

$$\frac{\partial c_0}{\partial S_0} + 1 = N(d_1) + 1 \text{ (from the Black-Scholes model)}$$

8.9)

The following data is given: $S_0 = \$50$, u $=1.1$, d $= 0.9$, $r_f = 2\%$. We need to price a put with K=50 and n=2. The stock takes the following values:

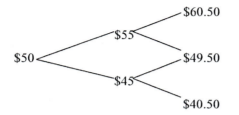

The tree diagram for the put is:

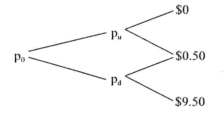

We can solve this problem using the risk neutral approach. First value the option assuming it is a European put, and then value it as an American option. The risk neutral probabilities are computed as follows:

$$\pi = \frac{1+r_f-d}{u-d} = \frac{1+0.02-0.9}{1.1-0.9} = \frac{0.12}{0.2} = 0.6$$

The European put values at each node are, respectively:

$$p_u^E = \frac{\$0 \times 0.6 + \$0.50 \times (1-0.6)}{1+0.02} = \$0.1961$$

$$p_d^E = \frac{\$0.50 \times 0.6 + \$9.50 \times (1-0.6)}{1+0.02} = \$4.0196$$

$$p_0^E = \frac{\$0.1961 \times 0.6 + \$4.0196 \times (1-0.6)}{1+0.02} = \$1.6917$$

Since an American option can be exercised early, check at each node to determine whether early exercise yields a higher payoff than keeping the option alive. The only node for which early exercise could be attractive is node d. Here, early exercise is optimal since early exercise yields ($\$50 - \$45$) = $\$5$ while the option is worth $\$4.02$.

Hence the value of the American put is:

$$p_0^A = \frac{\$0.1961 \times 0.6 + \$5 \times (1-0.6)}{1+0.02} = \$2.08$$

8.10)

We have $S_{Sure} = \$50$, $c_{Sure}(X = 50, T = 0.75) = \$3$, and $S_{Steady} = \$50$, $c_{Steady}(X = 50, T = 0.75) = \$3$. Since the options have the same characteristics (stock price, exercise price and time to maturity) and price, it must be the case that volatility is the same for each of the two stocks. At the merger, one share of either can be exchanged for one share of Sure and Steady. In the absence of synergies, Sure and Steady Corp. should sell for the same \$50 per share.

The difference between the exercise price of the option and the current value of the stock would remain unchanged, as would the maturity and the risk-free rate. The key variable affecting the option value is the volatility of the underlying stock. However the stock of the merged company will be more diversified and less volatile than the stock of each of the combined units considered independently. If volatility decreases as a consequence of the merger, the value of the options decreases.

The same analysis can be extended to analyze the impact of mergers on the value of equity in levered firms. The equity in a levered firm can be thought of as a call option on the underlying assets of the firm, with exercise price equal to the amount to be repaid on the debt and expiration date equal to the maturity date of the debt. Since the merger reduces the overall volatility of the assets of the firm, it also reduces the value of the equity.

8.11)

MV assets $(A) = \$1$ million, $\sigma_A = 0.30$, Debt $(D) = \$1$ million face value, $rf = 0.05$

The value of the equity is equal to the value of a call with a strike price of \$1 million.

$$PV\,(D) = \frac{\$1\,\text{million}}{1.05} = \$0.952\,\text{million}$$

According to the Black-Scholes model:

$$\text{Equity} = A \times N\left\{\frac{\ln[A/PV(D)]}{\sigma\sqrt{T}} + \frac{\sigma\sqrt{T}}{2}\right\} - PV(D) \times N\left\{\frac{\ln[A/PV(D)]}{\sigma\sqrt{T}} - \frac{\sigma\sqrt{T}}{2}\right\}$$

$$= \$1,000,000 \times N\left\{\frac{\ln(1,050,000)}{.30\sqrt{1}} + \frac{.30\sqrt{1}}{2}\right\}$$

$$- \$952,000 \times N\left\{\frac{\ln(1,050,000)}{.30\sqrt{1}} - \frac{.30\sqrt{1}}{2}\right\}$$

$$= \$1\,\text{million} \times N(0.313) - \$0.952\,\text{million} \times N(0.013)$$
$$= \$1\,\text{million}(.623) - \$0.952\,\text{million}(.505)$$
$$= \$0.142240\,\text{million}$$

$\therefore MV$ equity $= \$142,240$

MV debt $= \$1$ million $- \$142,240 = \$857,760$

8.12)

    Chrysler Corporation received loan guarantees from the U.S. government (i.e., in the event that Chrysler would become bankrupt, the U.S. Treasury would have had to pay Chrysler's creditors). In exchange, the government received a senior claim on the assets of the firm and warrants for the purchase of Chrysler's stock.

    By providing the loan guarantees, the government effectively made Chrysler's debt risk free. However, the senior claim on Chrysler's assets did not eliminate the risk the government faced. If the value of Chrysler's assets had been high enough when the debt matured, Chrysler would have repaid its debt in full and kept ownership of the assets. If the assets' value declined below the promised debt repayment, Chrysler would have filed for bankruptcy, the government would have had to repay the debt in full and would have gained ownership of Chrysler's assets as a result of the senior claim on the assets. However, at that time, those assets would have had a value less than the amount the government would have paid in order to repay the debt. Hence, the granting of the guarantees did entail significant risk for the government, even with the senior claim on the assets. Thus, the warrants were not a gift, but rather they were compensation for the risk, borne by the government, that the assets would be insufficient to repay the debt. In order to determine whether this compensation was reasonable, one would value both the guarantee and the warrants to see whether they are equivalent.

8.13)

$\frac{\partial c_0}{\partial S_0}$ is the number of shares of stock needed in the tracking portfolio for a call.

Since $\frac{\partial c_0}{\partial S_0} > 0$ then:

(i) if $S_0 \uparrow \Rightarrow \frac{\partial c_0}{\partial S_0} \uparrow \Rightarrow$ the number of shares of stock in the tracking portfolio increases.

(ii) if $S_0 \downarrow \Rightarrow \frac{\partial c_0}{\partial S_0} \downarrow \Rightarrow$ the number of shares of stock in the tracking portfolio decreases.

Similarly, since $\frac{\partial p_0}{\partial S_0} < 0$ then:

(i) if $S_0 \uparrow \Rightarrow \frac{\partial p_0}{\partial S_0} \downarrow \Rightarrow$ the number of shares of stock in the tracking portfolio decreases.

(ii) if $S_0 \downarrow \Rightarrow \frac{\partial p_0}{\partial S_0} \downarrow \Rightarrow$ the number of shares of stock in the tracking portfolio increases.

8.14)

A callable bond is a bond that can be repaid prior to maturity, at a pre-specified premium, at the option of the issuing company. The call feature is valuable to the issuing company if interest rates decrease and the debt can be refinanced at a significantly lower rate than the rate paid on the bond. Callable bonds generally carry a higher interest rate than comparable non-callable debt in order to compensate investors for the option granted to the borrower. Callable bonds are generally priced as if the issuer will optimally exercise the call option. If the issuer systematically does not exercise optimally (i.e., waits too long before calling the bonds), then the option is worth less than if exercised optimally, and the bond is worth more than if the option were exercised optimally. Hence, callable bonds are usually underpriced. To take advantage of this arbitrage opportunity, buy the bond and sell a tracking portfolio of the stock and the riskless asset. The tracking portfolio should be based on the optimal call policy for the bond.

8.15)

a)

Between dates 1 and 2, the risk-free rate is 15%. For the upper portion of the tree diagram, the risk neutral probabilities are given by the solution to the following equation:

$$\frac{30\pi + 10(1-\pi)}{1.15} = 20$$

$$\pi = 0.65$$

For the lower portion of the tree diagram between dates 1 and 2, the risk neutral probabilities are given by the solution to the following equation:

$$\frac{10\pi + 6(1-\pi)}{1.15} = 8$$

$$\pi = 0.80$$

One period earlier, with a risk-free rate of 12%, the risk neutral probabilities are given by the solution to the following equation:

$$\frac{20\pi + 8(1-\pi)}{1.12} = 12.50$$

$$\pi = 0.50$$

b)

The date 2 payoffs are:

for two up moves: $30 – 8 = 22
for an up move and a down move: $10 - $8 = 2
for two down moves: $0

c)

At the date 1 up node, the value of the call is:

$$\frac{\$22 \times 0.65 + \$2 \times (1 - 0.65)}{1.15} = \$13.04$$

At the date 1 down node, the value of the call is:

$$\frac{\$2 \times 0.8 + \$0 \times (1 - 0.8)}{1.15} = \$1.39$$

Therefore, at date 0, the value of the call is:

$$\frac{\$13.04 \times 0.5 + \$1.39 \times (1 - 0.5)}{1.12} = \$6.44$$

8.16)   [Note: In the first printing of the second edition, this exercise should read, "with a strike price *that has a present value* of $28."]

a)

$$c_0 = \$30 \times N\left[\frac{\ln\left(\$30/\$28\right)}{0.20\sqrt{0.25}} + \frac{0.20\sqrt{0.25}}{2}\right] - \$28 \times N\left[\frac{\ln\left(\$30/\$28\right)}{0.20\sqrt{0.25}} - \frac{0.20\sqrt{0.25}}{2}\right]$$

$$= \$30 \times N(0.7399) - \$28 \times N(0.6399) = \$30(0.7703) - \$28(0.7389) = \$2.4198$$

b)

The stock under consideration here is a stock that does not pay dividends. For nondividend-paying stocks, the right of premature exercise would never be used so the price of the option would not be higher if the call were American.

c)

For a stock that pays dividends, there are some situations where premature exercise is more valuable than waiting. Therefore, the American option would be more valuable than the comparable European option.

CHAPTER 9
DISCOUNTING AND VALUATION

9.1)

a)

	0	1	2	3	4	5	6
Time 1 perpetuity	0	C	$C(1+g)$	$C(1+g)^2$	$C(1+g)^3$	$C(1+g)^4$	$C(1+g)^5$
Time 0 perpetuity	C	$C(1+g)$	$C(1+g)^2$	$C(1+g)^3$	$C(1+g)^4$	$C(1+g)^5$	$C(1+g)^6$

So the cash flow for the time 0 perpetuity at each date ($t = 1$ onwards) is $(1+g)$ times the cash flow for the time 1 perpetuity.

b)

The PV of the time 0 perpetuity is $(1+r)$ times the PV of the time 1 perpetuity. If we shift each cash flow of the time 1 perpetuity backward in time by one period, each cash flow is $(1+r)$ times as valuable.

c)

At time 0, CF(time 0 perpetuity) = C

CF(time 1 perpetuity) = 0

In addition to this difference of C at time 0, the time 0 perpetuity is $(1+g)$ times the time 1 perpetuity for each date from $t = 1$ onwards.

d)

The time 0 perpetuity's present value is $[C + PV \times (1+g)]$, where PV is the present value of the time 1 perpetuity.

e)

$C + [PV \times (1+g)] = PV \times (1+r)$

$$PV = \frac{C}{r - g}$$

9.2)

If compounded semiannually, find t as follows, where $[P \times (1+.04)^t] = 2P$:

$t = \ln(2)/\ln(1.04) = 17.6730$ (periods)

So it takes about 8.84 years to double your money.

If compounded annually: $[P \times (1+.08)^t] = 2P$ so that:

$t = \ln(2)/\ln(1.08) = 9.0065$ (periods)

So, with less frequent compounding it takes just over 9 years to double your money.

9.3)

The monthly rate is (9%/12) =0.75%

PV of mortgage =

$$\frac{C}{r} - \frac{C}{r}\left(\frac{1}{1+r}\right)^T = \frac{C}{r}\left(1-\left(\frac{1}{1+r}\right)^T\right) = \frac{1,500}{0.0075}\left(1-\left(\frac{1}{1+0.0075}\right)^{360}\right) = \$186,422.80$$

Purchase price = (PV of mortgage) $\times$ (1+.20) = \$223,707.36

9.4)

Solve for r, where: $[1+(0.10/2)^2] = (1 + \frac{r}{365})^{365}$

r = 0.097593

So the annualized interest rate, compounded daily, is 9.7593%.

$$(1+\frac{r}{365})^{365} = e^{10\% \times 1} = e^{0.10}$$

r = 0.100014

A 10% continuously compounded interest rate is equivalent to a 10.0014% annualized interest rate, compounded daily.

9.5)

The present value, on his 65th birthday, of the 360-month annuity is computed with the following formula:

$$PV = \frac{C}{r}\left(1-\left(\frac{1}{1+r}\right)^T\right)$$

For T=360, r = (0.07/12), C=\$2,000, then PV = \$300,615.14

The value, at age 34, of his annual deposit of D is computed with the following formula:

$$\frac{D}{r}\left[1 - \frac{1}{(1+r)^T}\right]$$

For r = .08 and T =30, then the value is 11.25778D

The value of (11.25778D), 31 years later, at 8% interest, is: $[11.25778D(1.08)^{31}]$ = 122.3458D

The after-tax investment value is:

$(122.3458D - 30D)(1 - 0.3) + 30D$

Setting this equal to the required need at age 65 calculated above and solving for D:

$(122.3458D - 30D)(1 - 0.3) + 30D = \$300,615.14$

$\Rightarrow$ D = \$3,176.34

He must deposit \$3,176.34 annually in order to achieve his expected retirement income.

9.6)

$$PV = \frac{C}{r} \times \frac{1}{(1+r)^{t-1}}$$

9.7)

Since the present value of the two mortgages is the same, solve for r where:

$$\frac{C}{.10/12}\left(1-\left(\frac{1}{1+.10/12}\right)^{360}\right) = \frac{C}{r/12}\left(1-\left(\frac{1}{1+r/12}\right)^{180}\right)$$

r = .0662 = 6.62%

9.8)

Relation Between Annually Compounded Interest Rate and PV of Zero-Coupon Bond

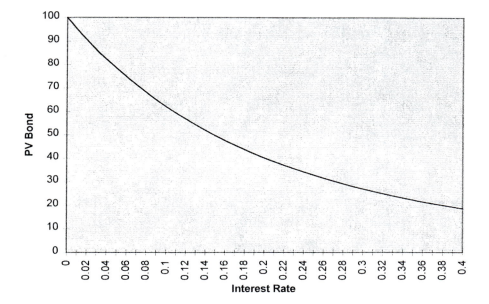

Relation Between Years to Maturity and PV of Zero-Coupon Bond (r = 8%)

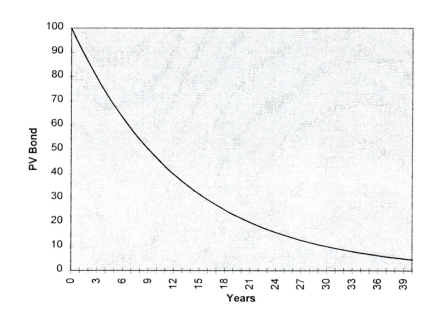

9.9)

$$P = \frac{C}{r - g} = \frac{\$2}{.07 - .03} = \$50$$

9.10)

The effective growth rate $g = (1 + .04)(1 + .01) - 1 = .0504$

$$\text{Compensation} = \frac{C}{r - g}\left(1 - \frac{(1 + g)^T}{(1 + r)^T}\right) = \frac{\$40,000}{.1000 - .0504}\left(1 - \frac{(1 + .0504)^{30}}{(1 + .10)^{30}}\right) = \$604,410.78$$

(This calculation is based on the assumption that the employee receives wages at the end of the year.)

9.11)

a)

For the simple monthly interest rate, solve for r where:

$(1 + 30r)(\$1000) = \$1212.50$

The annualized simple interest rate = $12(0.007083) = 8.50\%$

b)

Solve for r, where:

$(1+r)^{30/12} = 1.2125$ $r = 8.01\%$

$(1+\frac{r}{2})^{2 \times 5/2} = 1.2125$ $r = 7.86\%$

$(1+\frac{r}{4})^{4 \times 5/2} = 1.2125$ $r = 7.78\%$

$(1+\frac{r}{12})^{12 \times 5/2} = 1.2125$ $r = 7.73\%$

$e^{2.5r} = 1.2125$ $r = 7.71\%$

c)

The annually compounded rate is the largest because it has the lowest compounding frequency.

9.12)

$$\$9,600 = \frac{\$10,000}{1+(3/4)(r)} \qquad \text{so that:} \quad r = 5.56\%$$

9.13)

$1 + 8.50\% = 1.085$

$(1+\frac{8.33\%}{2})^2 = 1.085$

$(1+\frac{8.25\%}{4})^4 = 1.085$

$e^{8.16\%} = 1.085$

The rates are all the same, since all of the rates provide the same future value starting with the same amount of money.

9.14)

a)

$$PV = \frac{\$10,000}{(1+.09)^{7/12}} = \$9,509.72$$

b)

$$\text{Deposit} = \frac{\$9,509.72}{(1+.09)^{30/12}} = \$7,666.58$$

9.15)

Weekly cash flow = $150 − $45 = $105

Weekly rate = $(1.06)^{1/52} − 1 = 0.112\%$

$$PV = \frac{\$150 - \$45}{0.00112}\left(1 - \frac{1}{(1.00112)^{52}}\right) + \frac{\$450}{(1 + .06)} - \frac{\$350}{(1 + .06)^{9/12}}$$

$$= \$5301.16 + \$424.53 - \$335.03 = \$5390.66$$

Difference = PV − start-up costs = $5,390.66 − $1,000.00 = $4,390.66

9.16)

a)

$$PV = \frac{\$9,000}{1 + .075} + \frac{\$9,500}{(1 + .075)^{15/12}} + \frac{\$10,500}{(1 + .075)^{30/12}} + \frac{\$11,500}{(1 + .075)^{38/12}} = \$34,960.41$$

b)

$$PV = \frac{\$9,000}{(1 + \frac{.075}{2})^{2}} + \frac{\$9,500}{(1 + \frac{.075}{2})^{15/6}} + \frac{\$10,500}{(1 + \frac{.075}{2})^{30/6}} + \frac{\$11,500}{(1 + \frac{.075}{2})^{38/6}} = \$34,868.92$$

9.17)

a)

$\$13,328 = \$10,000\,(1+.09)^{t}$ $t = \dfrac{\ln(13,328/10,000)}{(1+.09)} = 3.3336$

b)

$\$13,328 = \$10,000(1+\frac{.09}{2})^{2t}$ $t = 3.2633$

c)

$\$13,328 = \$10,000\,(1+.11)^{t}$ $t = 2.7528$

9.18)

a)

(1) $\$350,000 + \dfrac{\$25,000}{(1 + .09)^{10}} = \$360,560.27$

(2) $\dfrac{\$42,500}{.09}\left(1 - \dfrac{1}{(1 + .09)^{20}}\right) = \$387,963.19$

(3) $\dfrac{\$35,000}{.09} = \$388,888.89$

Program 3 has the highest present value.

b)

(1) $\$350,000 + \dfrac{\$25,000}{(1+.10)^{10}} = \$359,638.58$

(2) $\dfrac{\$42,500}{0.10}\left(1 - \dfrac{1}{(1.10)^{20}}\right) = \$361,826.46$

(3) $\dfrac{\$35,000}{.10} = \$350,000$

Program 2 has the highest present value.

c)

(1) $\$350,000 + \dfrac{\$25,000}{(1+.11)^{10}} = \$358,804.61$

(2) $\dfrac{\$42,500}{0.11}\left(1 - \dfrac{1}{(1.11)^{20}}\right) = \$338,441.45$

(3) $\dfrac{\$35,000}{.11} = \$318,181.82$

Program 1 has the highest present value.

9.19)

a)

$$PV = C + \dfrac{C(1+g)}{r-g}\left(1 - \dfrac{(1+g)^{T}}{(1+r)^{T}}\right) = \$5000 + \dfrac{\$5,000(1+.04)}{.09-.04}\left(1 - \left(\dfrac{1+.04}{1+.09}\right)^{19}\right) = \$66,384.92$$

Since $\$66,384.92 < \$67,500$, choose to pay the annual premium.

b)

$$PV = C + \dfrac{C(1+g)}{r-g}\left(1 - \dfrac{(1+g)^{T}}{(1+r)^{T}}\right) = \$5000 + \dfrac{\$5,000(1+.04)}{.10-.04}\left(1 - \left(\dfrac{1+.04}{1+.10}\right)^{19}\right) = \$61,811.15$$

Since $\$61,811.15 < \$67,500$, choose to pay the annual premium.

c)

The PV of the annuity decreases as r increases.

9.20)

$$PV = \frac{\$2000}{(1+.07)^2(0.07)}\left(1-\frac{1}{(1+.07)^{12}}\right) + \frac{\$5000}{(1+.07)^{14}(0.07)}\left(1-\frac{1}{(1+.07)^8}\right) + \frac{\$3000}{(1+.07)^{22}(0.07)}$$

$$= \$13,874.90 + \$11,578.86 + \$9,673.42 = \$35,127.18$$

9.21)

a)

$$PV = \frac{1}{(1+.07)^{17}} \times \frac{(\$15,000)(1+.04)^{18}}{.07-.04}\left(1-\left(\frac{1.04}{1.07}\right)^4\right) = \$34,477.61$$

b)

Solve for C where: $\dfrac{C}{.07}\left(1-\dfrac{1}{(1+.07)^{18}}\right) = \$34,477.61$

C = $3,427.51

9.22)

a)

PV on your 65th birthday $= \dfrac{\$50,000}{.08-.04}\left(1-\left(\dfrac{1.04}{1.08}\right)^{10}\right) = \$392,950.61$

Future value at 65th birthday: $FV = \dfrac{C}{.08}\left(1-\dfrac{1}{(1+.08)^{30}}\right)(1+.08)^{30} = \$392,950.61$

Therefore: C = $3,468.75

b)

$$PV = \frac{\$50,000}{.09-.04}\left(1-\left(\frac{1.04}{1.09}\right)^{10}\right) = \$374,728.82$$

$$C = \frac{(\$374,728.82)(0.09)}{(1.09^{30}-1)} = \$2,749.14$$

So the required annual deposit decreases.

c)

$$\$374,728.82 = \frac{C}{.09-.04}\left(1-\left(\frac{1.04}{1.09}\right)^{20}\right) \Rightarrow C = \$30,764.10$$

9.23)

	Q1	Q2	Q3	Q4	Q1	Q2	Q3	Q4	Q1	Q2	Q3	Q4
CF1	3,000				3,000				3,000			
CF2		4,000				4,000				4,000		
CF3			5,000				5,000				5,000	
CF4				6,000				6,000				6,000

a)

$$\text{PV for CF1} = \frac{\$3,000}{.10}(1.10)^{3/4} = \$32,222.99$$

$$\text{PV for CF2} = \frac{\$4,000}{.10}(1.10)^{1/2} = \$41,952.35$$

$$\text{PV for CF3} = \frac{\$5,000}{.10}(1.10)^{1/4} = \$51,205.68$$

$$\text{PV for CF4} = \frac{\$6,000}{.10} = \$60,000$$

TOTAL PV = $185,381.02

b)

$$\text{PV for CF1} = \frac{\$3,000}{.10-.01}(1.10)^{3/4} = \$35,803.32$$

$$\text{PV for CF2} = \frac{\$4,000}{.10-.01}(1.10)^{1/2} = \$46,613.73$$

$$\text{PV for CF3} = \frac{\$5,000}{.10-.01}(1.10)^{1/4} = \$56,895.20$$

$$\text{PV for CF4} = \frac{\$6,000}{.10-.01} = \$66,666.67$$

TOTAL PV = $205,978.92

c)

$$\text{PV for CF1} = \frac{\$3,000(1.10)^{3/4}}{.10-.01}\left(1-\frac{(1.01)^{10}}{(1.10)^{10}}\right) + \frac{\$3,000}{.10}\frac{(1.01)^9}{(1.10)^{10}}(1.10)^{3/4}$$

$$= \$20,555.41 + \$13,587.24 = \$34,142.65$$

$$\text{PV for CF2} = \frac{\$4,000(1.10)^{1/2}}{.10-.01}\left(1-\frac{(1.01)^{10}}{(1.10)^{10}}\right) + \frac{\$4,000}{.10}\frac{(1.01)^9}{(1.10)^{10}}(1.10)^{1/2}$$

$$= \$26,761.89 + \$17,689.76 = \$44,451.65$$

$$\text{PV for CF3} = \frac{\$5,000(1.10)^{1/4}}{.10-.01}\left(1-\frac{(1.01)^{10}}{(1.10)^{10}}\right)+\frac{\$5,000}{.10}\frac{(1.01)^9}{(1.10)^{10}}(1.10)^{1/4}$$

$$= \$32,664.70 + \$21,591.54 = \$54,256.24$$

$$\text{PV for CF4} = \frac{\$6,000}{.10-.01}\left(1-\frac{(1.01)^{10}}{(1.10)^{10}}\right)+\frac{\$6,000}{.10}\frac{(1.01)^9}{(1.10)^{10}}$$

$$= \$38,274.69 + \$25,299.78 = \$63,574.47$$

TOTAL PV = $196,425.01

9.24)

Month	Monthly rate	Periods remaining	Monthly payment	Interest paid	Principal paid	Principal balance
0						$100,000.00
1	0.0058333	360	$665.30	$583.33	$81.97	$ 99,918.03
2	0.0059375	359	$673.71	$593.26	$80.45	$ 99,837.58
3	0.0060417	358	$682.14	$603.19	$78.95	$ 99,758.63

9.25)

No, the $100,000 does not represent a reduction in the unlevered cash flows generated by the project. The CEO will be paid regardless of whether super secret project X is adopted. Hence, if we look at the difference between the unlevered cash flows of the firm with and without project X, none of the difference can be attributed to the CEO's salary.

9.26)

Year	EBIT	Depreciation	EBITDA	Increase in Working Capital	Pretax Cash Flow	Taxes (at 40%)	Unlevered Cash Flow
1	$10,000.00	$100,000.00	$110,000.00	$10,000.00	$100,000.00	$4,000.00	$96,000.00
2	12,200.00	100,000.00	112,200.00	10,200.00	102,000.00	4,880.00	97,120.00
3	14,444.00	100,000.00	114,444.00	10,404.00	104,040.00	5,777.60	98,262.40
4	16,732.88	100,000.00	116,732.88	10,612.08	106,120.80	6,693.15	99,427.65
5	19,067.54	100,000.00	119,067.54	10,824.32	108,243.22	7,627.02	100,616.20
6	121,448.89	0.00	121,448.89	11,040.81	110,408.08	48,579.56	61,828.52
7	123,877.87	0.00	123,877.87	11,261.62	112,616.24	49,551.15	63,065.10
8	126,355.42	0.00	126,355.42	11,486.86	114,868.57	50,542.17	64,326.40

Depreciation expense in column (b) does not change because it is based on straight-line depreciation of the asset's initial nominal value. Hence, nominal depreciation for tax purposes is not affected by inflation.

9.27)

$$PV = \frac{\$96,000}{(1.10)^1} + \frac{\$97,120}{(1.10)^2} + \frac{\$98,262.40}{(1.10)^3} + \frac{\$99,427.65}{(1.10)^4}$$

$$+ \frac{\$100,616.20}{(1.10)^5} + \frac{\$61,828.52}{(1.10)^6} + \frac{\$63,065.10}{(1.10)^7} + \frac{\$64,326.40}{(1.10)^8} = \$469,020.05$$

9.28)

Year	EBIT	Depreciation	EBITDA	Increase in Working Capital	Pretax Cash Flow	Taxes (at 40%)	Unlevered Cash Flow
1	$9,803.92	$98,039.22	$107,843.14	$9,803.92	$98,039.22	$3,921.57	$94,117.65
2	11,726.26	96,116.88	107,843.14	9,803.92	98,039.22	4,690.50	93,348.71
3	13,610.90	94,232.23	107,843.14	9,803.92	98,039.22	5,444.36	92,594.85
4	15,458.59	92,384.54	107,843.14	9,803.92	98,039.22	6,183.44	91,855.78
5	17,270.06	90,573.08	107,843.14	9,803.92	98,039.22	6,908.02	91,131.19
6	107,843.14	0.00	107,843.14	9,803.92	98,039.22	43,137.25	54,901.96
7	107,843.14	0.00	107,843.14	9,803.92	98,039.22	43,137.25	54,901.96
8	107,843.14	0.00	107,843.14	9,803.92	98,039.22	43,137.25	54,901.96

a) real discount rate = $(1.10/1.02) - 1 = 7.843137\%$

b)

$$PV = \frac{\$94,117.65}{(1.07843137)^1} + \frac{\$93,348.71}{(1.07843137)^2} + \frac{\$92,594.85}{(1.07843137)^3} + \frac{\$91,855.78}{(1.07843137)^4}$$

$$+ \frac{\$91,131.19}{(1.07843137)^5} + \frac{\$54,901.96}{(1.07843137)^6} + \frac{\$54,901.96}{(1.07843137)^7} + \frac{\$54,901.96}{(1.07843137)^8} = \$469,020.05$$

9.29)

The answer to this exercise changes with each new set of financial statements for ExxonMobil. Use the template from Example 9.1 and the most recent financial statements for ExxonMobil, which can be obtained from the following web site: http://www.sec.gov/edgar.shtml

10.1)

a)

Cash flows ($ millions) at year:

	0	1	2	3	4	5	NPV($millions)	Profitability
Northeast	-95	15	20	25	30	30	- 0.157760	0.99
Midwest	-75	15	20	20	25	30	12.016748 profitable	1.16
Southeast	-60	10	15	20	20	25	10.807800 profitable	1.18
West Coast	-35	5	10	10	15	15	8.032958 profitable	1.23
Southwest	-20	5	5	6	6	10	5.258452 profitable	1.26
Zero coupon yields:		6.5%	7.0%	7.0%	7.5%	8.0%		

The most profitable region is the Midwest.

b)

The optimal combination of programs is to expand into the Southeast and West Coast, which will cost $95 million, but will yield an NPV of $18.841 million.

c)

Without regional saturation, choose five expansions in the Southwest region with profit equal to $26.292 million. Note that the Southwest has the largest profitability index.

10.2)

Cash Flows (in $000s)

Sale of
Old Machine   *Savings in Operating Expenses*

t=0	1	2	3	4	5	6	7	8	9	10
20	20	20	20	20	20	20	20	20	20	20

$$PV = \$20,000 + \sum_{t=1}^{10} \frac{\$20,000}{(1.10)^t} = \$142,891$$

Thus for the NPV of the project to be zero, the price of the new milling machine must equal $142,891.

10.3)

a)

Incremental cash flows in $ at:

Year 0	Year 1	Year 2	Year 3	Year 4	Year 5
−40	−10	15	20	15	13

These figures represent cash inflows. The positive cash inflows represent positive revenue, and the negative inflows imply positive cash outflows or costs at years 0 and 1.

b)

$$PV = \frac{-\$10}{1.08} + \frac{\$15}{(1.08)^2} + \frac{\$20}{(1.08)^3} + \frac{\$15}{(1.08)^4} + \frac{\$13}{(1.08)^5} = \$39.35$$

c)

Given the flat term structure, the hurdle rate is 8%. The IRR is lower than the hurdle rate in this case. This is because, at 8%, NPV < 0, and we have a later cash flow stream, which means that if $r > 8\%$ then NPV is always negative. Thus IRR must be less than 8% for the NPV to equal 0.

d)

A flat rate structure is unrealistic because long-maturity bonds always have yield-to-maturity different from the yield-to-maturity of short-maturity riskless bonds. This means that there are different discount rates for cash flows of different time horizons.

10.4)

Tracking portfolio for project X:
1) Issue (short) zero coupon bonds maturing in 1 year with aggregate FV=$10 at a cost of $0.926 per $1 of face value.
2) Purchase zero coupon bonds maturing in 2 years with aggregate FV = $15 at a cost of $0.857 per $1 of face value.
3) Purchase zero coupon bonds maturing in 3 years with aggregate FV = $20 at a cost of $0.794 per $1 of face value.
4) Purchase zero coupon bonds maturing in 4 years with aggregate FV = $15 at a cost of $0.735 per $1 of face value.
5) Purchase zero coupon bonds maturing in 5 years with aggregate FV = $13 at a cost of $0.681 per $1 of face value.

Hence, at an 8% discount rate, the aggregate cost of the tracking portfolio is $39.35.
We are interested in tracking with a portfolio of marketable securities because they represent the amount the financial markets are willing to pay for identical cash flow streams when cash flows are certain. Valuation based on tracking can be used to measure the arbitrage profit created by the real investment when financed with a short position in the tracking portfolio.

10.5)

FV = $100, B_1 = $94.00, B_2 = $88.20, B_3 = $81.50, B_4 = $76.00, B_5 = $73.00

a)

Solve for r in the following equation: $1 + r_t = \left[\frac{100}{B_t}\right]^{\frac{1}{t}}$

$$1 + r_1 = \frac{\$100.00}{\$94.00} \Rightarrow r_1 = 6.38\%$$

$$(1+r_2)^2 = \frac{\$100.00}{\$88.20} \Rightarrow r_2 = 6.48\%$$

$$(1+r_3)^3 = \frac{\$100.00}{\$81.50} \Rightarrow r_3 = 7.06\%$$

$$(1+r_4)^4 = \frac{\$100.00}{\$76.00} \Rightarrow r_4 = 7.10\%$$

$$(1+r_5)^5 = \frac{\$100.00}{\$73.00} \Rightarrow r_5 = 6.50\%$$

b)

Asset portfolio from Exercise 10.4:

$$PV = -\$10(\frac{1}{1.0638}) + \$15(\frac{1}{1.0648^2}) + \$20(\frac{1}{1.0706^3}) + \$15(\frac{1}{1.0710^4}) + \$13(\frac{1}{1.0650^5})$$

$$= \$41.02$$

c)

$$NPV(X) = -\$40 + \frac{-\$10}{1.0638} + \frac{\$15}{(1.0648)^2} + \frac{\$20}{(1.0706)^3} + \frac{\$15}{(1.0710)^4} + \frac{\$13}{(1.0650)^5} = \$1.02$$

d)

Part (b) provides the cost of the tracking portfolio for project X given the zero coupon bond prices for this problem. This present value represents the cost, in the financial markets, of producing future cash flows equal to those provided by the project. The wealth created because the firm produces these cash flows at a lower cost is: $41.02 - $40.00 = $1.02. This is the same as the NPV.

10.6)

a)

Cash flows for project X are a "later cash flow stream."

b)

Since PV = $41.02, find r such that:

$$\$0 = -\$41.02 + \frac{-\$10}{1+r} + \frac{\$15}{(1+r)^2} + \frac{\$20}{(1+r)^3} + \frac{\$15}{(1+r)^4} + \frac{\$13}{(1+r)^5} \Rightarrow r = 6.85\%$$

This represents the rate above which the project will be profitable. If the IRR > hurdle rate, then NPV > 0 (i.e., accept the project).

c)

$$\$0 = -\$40 + \frac{-\$10}{1+IRR} + \frac{\$15}{(1+IRR)^2} + \frac{\$20}{(1+IRR)^3} + \frac{\$15}{(1+IRR)^4} + \frac{\$13}{(1+IRR)^5} \Rightarrow IRR = 7.54\%$$

d)

Since $IRR\% = 7.54\% > 6.85\%$ = hurdle rate, accept the project.

e)

If the sign of each cash flow is reversed, the hurdle rate and the IRR do not change, but now, since we have an early cash flow stream, we should accept projects for which the hurdle rate exceeds the IRR. Thus, in this case, since IRR > hurdle rate, we reject the project with reversed cash flows.

10.7)

a)

t:	0	1	2	3	4	5
Project 1	−40	10	10	15	15	20
Project 2	−25	5	5	10	15	15
Project 3	−20	5	5	5	10	15
Project 4	−15	3	3	6	6	13
Zero Coupon Yields		5%	5%	6%	6%	5%

	NPV	Hurdle Rate	IRR
Project 1	18.740	5.55%	19.22%
Project 2	16.328	5.50%	22.43%
Project 3	13.169	5.38%	22.52%
Project 4	10.554	5.37%	22.72%

Project 1 appears to be the most promising because it has the largest NPV.

b)

t:	0	1	2	3	4	5	NPV
Project 1	−15	5	5	5	0	5	2.413
Project 2	15	−5	−5	−5	0	−5	−2.413
Project 3	20	−5	−5	−10	−5	−5	−5.571
Project 4	25	−7	−7	−9	−9	−7	−8.186

Therefore, accept only Project 1.

c)

If the projects are scalable:

t:	0	1	2	3	4	5
Project 1	−40	10	10	15	15	20
Project 2	−25	5	5	10	15	15
Project 3	−20	5	5	5	10	15
Project 4	−15	3	3	6	6	13

	NPV	Profitability Index
Project 1	18.740	1.469
Project 2	16.328	1.653
Project 3	13.169	1.658
Project 4	10.554	1.704

Since Project 4 has the highest profitability index, and all projects are scalable, use Project 4 three and one-third times. This provides an NPV of $35.18 million.

10.8)

a)

The least common horizon is 12 years.

year	Machine 1	Machine 2	Machine 3
0	2000	3200	4500
1	400	300	200
2	2400	300	200
3	400	3500	200
4	2400	300	4700
5	400	300	200
6	2400	3500	200
7	400	300	200
8	2400	300	4700
9	400	3500	200
10	2400	300	200
11	400	300	200
12	400	300	200
NPV(@5%)	$13,078.70	$13,073.89	**$13,020.59**
NPV(@6%)	**$12,499.25**	$12,551.88	$12,564.55

b)

Under a flat term structure of 5%, Machine 3 makes the most sense from a cost efficiency standpoint. The present value of its costs is the lowest because more of the cost of Machine 3 occurs in earlier years.

c)

Under a flat term structure of 6%, Machine 1 makes the most sense from a cost efficiency standpoint. The present value of its costs is the lowest because more of the cost of Machine 1 occurs in later years.

10.9)

a)

The least common horizon is six years.

Alternatives	0	1	2	3	4	5	6	NPV
A+A+A	−2.5	1.5	−1.0	1.5	−1.0	1.5	1.5	0.5918
B+B	−3.5	1.7	1.7	−1.8	1.7	1.7	1.7	1.8552
Zero-coupon rates:	5.0%	5.5%	6.0%	6.0%	6.5%	7.0%		

b)

The optimal decision is to acquire technology B at time 0 and then replace it with technology B again at time 3.

c)

For B+B, the present value of the costs incurred in years 0 and 3 is −$6.4387 million, and the present value of the revenues in years 1 through 6 is $8.2939 million. In order for B+B to have the same NPV as A+A+A (i.e., $0.5918 million), the present value of the cost must be equal to the NPV ($.5918 million) minus the present value of the revenues ($8.2939 million), or −$7.7021 million. A cost of −$4.1868 million in year 0 and year 3 results in a present value of costs equal to −$7.7021 million, and therefore in a net present value of $0.5918 million. Therefore, if the cost of package B is $4.1868 million, then Investco would be indifferent between the two packages.

Appendix

10A.1)

 a)

 $B_1 = 100/1.08^2 = \$85.73$

 $B_2 = 100/1.10^2 = \$82.64$

 b)

t=0	t=1	t=2
-$82.64	$0	$100
$85.73	$0	-$100
$ 3.09	$0	$ 0

 c)

Yes, these cash flows are indicative of arbitrage because you receive $3.09 today for a riskless zero cash flow position in the future.

 d)

Since the future position is now uncertain, this is not necessarily indicative of arbitrage. The same arbitrage strategy described in part (c) will require a payment of $100 in 2 years and a receipt of $100 in 3 years.

10A.2)

 To calculate the annuity yields, solve for r_1, r_2, and r_3 in the following equations:

$$\frac{1}{1+r_1} = \frac{1}{1.045} = 0.95694$$

$$\frac{1}{1+r_2} + \frac{1}{(1+r_2)^2} = \frac{1}{1.045} + \frac{1}{1.05^2} = 1.86397$$

$$\frac{1}{1+r_3} + \frac{1}{(1+r_3)^2} + \frac{1}{(1+r_3)^3} = \frac{1}{1.045} + \frac{1}{1.05^2} + \frac{1}{1.0525^3} = 2.72166$$

The solution is: $r_1 = 4.500\%$, $r_2 = 4.827\%$, $r_3 = 5.031\%$

The par yields for years 1, 2, and 3 are computed as follows:

$$\text{year 1:} \quad \frac{\$100 - \dfrac{\$100}{1.045}}{\$0.95694} = 4.50\%$$

$$\text{year 2:} \quad \frac{\$100 - \dfrac{\$100}{1.05^2}}{\$1.86397} = 4.99\%$$

$$\text{year 3:} \quad \frac{\$100 - \dfrac{\$100}{1.0525^3}}{\$2.72166} = 5.23\%$$

10A.3)

To calculate the spot yields, solve for r_1, r_2, r_3 and r_4 in the following equations:

$r_1 = 4.500\%$

$$100 - \frac{5}{1.045} = \frac{105}{(1+r_2)^2} \quad \text{so that} \quad \longrightarrow \quad r_2 = 5.013\%$$

$$100 - \frac{5.25}{1.045} - \frac{5.25}{1.05013^2} = \frac{105.25}{(1+r_3)^3} \quad \text{so that} \quad \longrightarrow r_3 = 5.272\%$$

$$100 - \frac{5.25}{1.045} - \frac{5.25}{1.05013^2} - \frac{5.25}{1.05272^3} = \frac{105.25}{(1+r_4)^4} \quad \text{so that} \quad \longrightarrow r_4 = 5.267\%$$

To calculate the annuity yields, solve for r_1, r_2, r_3, and r_4 in the following equations:

$r_1 = 4.500\%$

$$\frac{1}{1+r_2} + \frac{1}{(1+r_2)^2} = \frac{1}{1.045} + \frac{1}{1.05013^2}$$

$$\frac{1}{1+r_3} + \frac{1}{(1+r_3)^2} + \frac{1}{(1+r_3)^3} = \frac{1}{1.045} + \frac{1}{1.05013^2} + \frac{1}{1.05272^3}$$

$$\frac{1}{1+r_4} + \frac{1}{(1+r_4)^2} + \frac{1}{(1+r_4)^3} + \frac{1}{(1+r_4)^4} = \frac{1}{1.045} + \frac{1}{1.05013^2} + \frac{1}{1.05272^3} + \frac{1}{1.05267^4}$$

The solution is: $r_1 = 4.500\%$, $r_2 = 4.836\%$, $r_3 = 5.046\%$, $r_4 = 5.130\%$

11.1)

Finding the certainty equivalent cash flow from Result (11.6), and discounting at r_f :

$$P_o = [1,000,000 - \frac{(250,000)(.05)(.5)}{(.05)^2}(.10-.05)]/1.05 = \$833,333.33$$

11.2)

$$E[C] = (.25)(\$40 \text{ million}) + (.50)(\$50 \text{ million}) + (.25)(\$60 \text{ million}) = \$50 \text{ million}$$

11.3)

The covariance between the cash flow and the return on the market can be decomposed as follows:

$$cov(C, R_m) = E[CR_m] - E[C] E[R_m]$$

$$E[CR_m] = (.25)(-.15)(\$40\text{million}) + (.50)(.05)(\$50\text{million}) + (.25)(.25)(\$60\text{million}) = \$3.5 \text{ million}$$

The expected return on the market is:

$$E(R_m) = (.25)(-.15) + (.50)(.05) + (.25)(.25) = 0.05$$

$$cov(C, R_m) = \$3.5 \text{ million} - (\$50 \text{ million})(.05) = \$1.0 \text{ million}$$

$$var(R_m) = E[R_m^2] - (E[R_m])^2 = \{(.25)(-.15)^2 + (.50)(.05)^2 + (.25)(.25)^2\} - (.05)^2 = 0.02$$

$$b_{CF} = \frac{cov(C, R_m)}{var(R_m)} = \frac{\$1.0 \text{ million}}{.02} = \$50 \text{ million}$$

11.4)

$$CE = \$50 \text{ million} - \frac{\$1.0 \text{ million}}{(.40)^2}(0.084) = \$49.475 \text{ million}$$

Historical data provides additional information about expected returns. Scenarios are subjective, while historical data is objective. The disadvantage of using historical data to forecast the future is that the past is not always the best indicator of the future.

11.5)

$$PV = \frac{\$49.475 \text{ million}}{1.04} = \$47.572 \text{ million}$$

11.6)

The expected market returns and standard deviations obtained from historical data are not exactly equal to the figures derived from the scenarios.

11.7)

Using equation (11.1):

$$PV = \frac{E(C)}{1 + r_f + \beta(\overline{R}_T - r_f)}$$

$$PV + PVr_f + PV\,\beta(\overline{R}_T - r_f) = E(C)$$

Since $b = \beta \times PV$ we can substitute for $(PV\beta)$ as follows:

$$PV(1 + r_f) + b(\overline{R}_T - r_f) = E(C)$$

$$PV = \frac{E(C) - b(\overline{R}_T - r_f)}{1 + r_f}$$

11.8)

a)

$$A_t - D_t = E_t$$

$100 million – $50 million = $50 million

$110 million – $50 million = $60 million

$$\% \text{ increase in value of equity} = \frac{\$60\,\text{million} - \$50\,\text{million}}{\$50\,\text{million}} = 20\%$$

b)

Assuming the interest rate on debt is zero, then:

$$\text{leverage ratio} = \frac{D}{E} = \frac{50}{60} = 0.833$$

11.9)

A negative cash flow beta implies that the cash flow of a project is negatively correlated with the market factor. Thus, when the market does well, the cash flows are low, and when the market is low, cash flows are high. In order to compute the certainty equivalent of a cash flow, we must subtract out the effect the market has on the value of those cash flows:

$$CE(C) = E[C] - b(E[R_m] - r_f)$$

CE is higher when b is negative since this cash flow provides a hedge; alternatively, the cash flow can be viewed as insurance against a downturn in the market.

Therefore, a cash flow that has a negative covariance with the market (i.e., $b < 0$) will have a certainty equivalent cash flow (CE) greater than its expected cash flow (E[C]).

11.10)

Comparison	β_E	D/E	$\beta_A = \frac{E}{D+E}\beta_E$
			$\beta_A = \frac{1}{(D/E)+1}\beta_E$
GM	1.20	0.40	0.8571
Lockheed	0.90	0.90	0.4737
Northrop	0.85	0.70	0.5000

11.11)

$$\beta_A^H = (\tfrac{1}{2})(0.4737) + (\tfrac{1}{2})(0.50) = 0.4869$$

11.12)

Using the CAPM:

$$E[r_{\text{Hughes}}] = 0.08 + (0.4869)(0.14 - 0.08) = 0.1092 = 10.92\%$$

11.13)

$$PV = \frac{E(C_1)}{r - g} = \frac{\$300\,\text{million}}{0.1092 - 0.05} = \$5,068\,\text{million}.$$

11.14)

Using GM's cost of capital instead:

$$E[r_{\text{GM}}] = 0.08 + (0.8571)(0.14 - 0.08) = 0.1314 = 13.14\%$$

$$PV = \frac{\$300\,\text{million}}{0.1314 - 0.05} = \$3,686\,\text{million}$$

11.15)

a)

$$E[r_{\text{HSCC}}] = r_f + \lambda_1\beta_1 + \lambda_2\beta_2$$
$$= 0.05 + (1.15)(0.02) + (-0.3)(-0.005) = 0.0745 = 7.45\%$$

b)

$$PV = \frac{E(C)}{1 + E[r_{\text{HSCC}}]} = \frac{\$1\,\text{million}}{1 + 0.0745} = \$0.931\,\text{million}$$

c)

$b_1 = \$1.07$ million

$b_2 = -\$0.28$ million

CE = [\$1 million – (\$1.07(0.02) – (\$0.28)(-0.005))]/1.05 = \$0.931 million

11.16)

$$\frac{\$200 \text{ million}}{1.06} = \$188.6792 \text{ million}$$

$$\frac{\$250 \text{ million}}{(1.0625)^2} = \$221.4533 \text{ million}$$

$$\frac{\$300 \text{ million}}{(1.0675)^3} = \$246.6139 \text{ million}$$

12.1)

By Result 12.6:

$$\frac{P_{M+W}}{NI_{M+W}} = w_M \frac{P_M}{NI_M} + w_W \frac{P_W}{NI_W} = (0.6)(20) + (1-0.6)(15) = 18$$

12.2)

The cash flows from the project (in $ millions) have the following tree diagram:

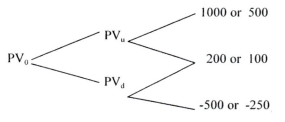

1000 or 500

200 or 100

-500 or -250

Using the formula $\pi = [(1+r_f - d)/(u - d)]$, the tree diagram for the risk neutral probabilities derived from the returns to investing in the market is:

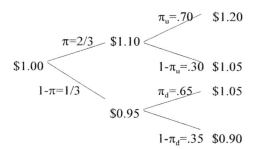

$\pi_u=.70$ $1.20

$\pi=2/3$ $1.10

$1.00

$1-\pi_u=.30$ $1.05

$1-\pi=1/3$

$\pi_d=.65$ $1.05

$0.95

$1-\pi_d=.35$ $0.90

a, b)[Note: the solution to (b) precedes the solution to (a).]

Let u define the up state and d the down state. Thus, there are four possible outcomes at date 2: uu, ud, du, and dd. Computing the value of the project without the scaling down option we have:

Step 1: Compute $PV_u(CF_2)$ (the present value at date 1 if the up state occurs):

$$PV_u(CF_2) = \frac{(\pi_u)(\$1000\ \text{million}) + (1-\pi_u)(\$200\ \text{million})}{1+r_f}$$

$$= \frac{(.70)(\$1000\ \text{million}) + (.30)(\$200\ \text{million})}{1+.05} = \$723.81\ \text{million}$$

Step 2: Compute $PV_d(CF_2)$ (the present value at date 1 if the down state occurs):

$$PV_d(CF_2) = \frac{(\pi_d)(\$200\ \text{million}) + (1-\pi_d)(-\$500\ \text{million})}{1+r_f}$$

$$= \frac{(.65)(\$200\ \text{million}) + (.35)(-\$500\ \text{million})}{1+.05} = -\$42.86\ \text{million}$$

Step 3: Compute $PV_0(CF_2)$ (the present value at date 0):

$$PV_0(CF_2) = \frac{(\pi)(\$723.81\,\text{million}) + (1-\pi)(-\$42.86\,\text{million})}{1+r_f}$$

$$= \frac{(2/3)(\$723.81\,\text{million}) + (1/3)(-\$42.86\,\text{million})}{1+.05}$$

$$= \$445.96\,\text{million}$$

Hence the NPV of the project without the scale down option is:

NPV = \$445.97 million – \$425.00 million = \$20.97 million

The scale down option will be exercised if the company finds itself in node d at the end of the first period, since the option reduces the potential losses much more than the potential gains. In the u state, since net cash flows 1 period later are uniformly positive, the scale down option will expire unexercised. So the payoff and the value PV_u remain unchanged.

Step 2 (scaled down): Compute $PV_d(CF_2)$:

$$PV_d(CF_2) = \frac{(.65)(\$100\,\text{million}) + (.35)(-\$250\,\text{million})}{1+.05} = -\$21.43\,\text{million}$$

Naturally, this is half the size of $PV_d(CF_2)$ in Step 2 above (without the option to scale down).

Step 3: Compute $PV_0(CF_2)$:

$$PV_0(CF_2) = \frac{(2/3)(\$723.81\,\text{million}) + (1/3)(-\$21.43\,\text{million})}{1+.05} = \$452.76\,\text{million}$$

Hence the NPV of the project with the scale down option is:

NPV = \$452.76 million – \$425.00 million = \$27.76 million.

Thus, the value of the scale down option is:

\$452.76 million – \$445.96 million = \$6.80 million

12.3)

a)

Since both house and condo values per square foot have to satisfy risk neutral valuation, we can specify the following two equations which can be solved for the risk neutral probabilities and the risk free rate:

$$\$225(1+r_f) = (\pi)[.10(\$225) + \$300] + (1-\pi)[.10(\$225) + \$200]$$

$$\$180(1+r_f) = (\pi)[.20(\$180) + \$230] + (1-\pi)[.20(\$180) + \$140]$$

The solution to the above equations is:

$$\pi = 0.20 \text{ and } r_f = 0.0778$$

b)

Now we can examine whether we should build condos or houses, and whether we should wait.

Building today:

If we build condos, the cash flow is: $(10,000) [\$180 - \$120] = \$600,000$

If we build houses, the cash flow is: $(2) (3,000) [\$225 - \$100] = \$750,000$

Therefore, if we build today, we should build houses.

Building next period:

If we build next period, the cash flows are as follows:

$$\max[(10,000)(\$230 - \$120), (2)(3,000)(\$300 - \$100)] = \$1,200,000$$

$$\max[(10,000)(\$140 - \$120), (2)(3,000)(\$200 - \$100)] = \$600,000$$

Using risk neutral valuation, we compute the PV of building either condos or houses next period:

$$PV_0 = \frac{(.20)(\$1,200,000) + (1 - .20)(\$600,000)}{1 + .0778} = \$668,027$$

Hence, since the cash flow from building today ($750,000) is larger than the PV of the cash flow from building next period ($668,027), building houses today is the optimal strategy.

The value of the vacant land is therefore $750,000.

12.4)

The certainty equivalent cash flows in each period are:

$$CE(C_0) = 10,000(\$4.00 - \$2.00) = \$20,000$$

$$CE(C_1) = 10,000(\$4.20 - \$2.00) = \$22,000$$

$$CE(C_2) = 5,000(\$4.50 - \$2.00) = \$12,500$$

Certainty equivalent cash flows are discounted at the risk free rate. Thus the value of the mine is:

$$V_0 = \$20,000 + \frac{\$22,000}{1.05} + \frac{\$12,500}{1.05^2} = \$52,290.25$$

12.5)

We are told that stock price changes in the widget industry are perfectly negatively correlated with changes in costs, and hence are perfectly positively correlated with cash flows (i.e., the market is in an up state when cash flows are high and vice versa). So the first step is to diagram the stock path and then to determine the costs and cash flows that correspond to each state in the stock value tree. The stock price diagram is as follows, given $u = 1.4$ and $d = 0.7$:

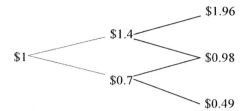

Given that $r_f = 12\%$, we can compute the risk neutral probabilities as follows:

$$\pi = \frac{(1+r_f)-d}{u-d} = \frac{(1+0.12)-0.7}{1.4-0.7} = 0.6$$

The cost of widget production follows a binomial process with up and down factors u = 0.5 and d = 1.5. Since stock values go down when costs go up, and stock values go up when costs go down, the tree diagram for the cost of widget production is:

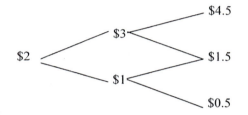

Given that the factory is shut down if production costs exceed resale prices, and that production is 1 million widgets per year and the resale price is $4 per widget, then the cash flows from operations are as follows:

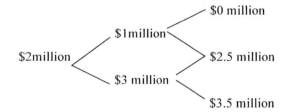

Then the values are:

$$V_{2,u} = \$3 \text{ million} + \frac{(.6)(\$3.5 \text{ million}) + (.4)(\$2.5 \text{ million})}{1.12} = \$5.77 \text{ million}$$

$$V_{2,d} = \$1 \text{ million} + \frac{.(6)(\$2.5 \text{ million}) + (.4)(\$0 \text{ million})}{1.12} = \$2.34 \text{ million}$$

$$V_1 = \$2 \text{ million} + \frac{(.6)(\$5.77 \text{ million}) + (.4)(\$2.34 \text{ million})}{1.12} = \$5.93 \text{ million}$$

$$V_0 = \frac{\$5.93 \text{ million}}{1.12} = \$5.29 \text{ million}$$

12.6)

The annual risk-free is 5%. Hence, the effective monthly risk-free discount rate is:

$$(1+.05)^{(1/12)} - 1 = 0.004074 = 0.4074\%$$

The following table summarizes the futures prices and certainty equivalent cash flows:

Month	Futures Price	Extraction Cost	Certainty Equivalent Cash Flow $(CE(C_t))$
Oct 02	$21.56	$2.00	$19,560
Nov 02	$21.08	$2.00	$19,080
Dec 02	$20.63	$2.00	$18,630
Jan 03	$20.23	$2.00	$18,230
Feb 03	$19.88	$2.00	$17,880
Mar 03	$19.55	$2.00	$17,550
Apr 03	$19.26	$2.00	$17,260
May 03	$19.00	$2.00	$17,000
Jun 03	$18.76	$2.00	$16,760
Jul 03	$18.58	$2.00	$16,580
Aug 03	$18.41	$2.00	$16,410
Sep 03	$18.25	$2.00	$16,250
Oct 03	$18.09	$2.00	$16,090
Nov 03	$17.93	$2.00	$15,930
Dec 03	$17.83	$2.00	$15,830
Jan 04	$17.77	$2.00	$15,770
Feb 04	$17.71	$2.00	$15,710
Mar 04	$17.66	$2.00	$15,660
Apr 04	$17.61	$2.00	$15,610
May 04	$17.56	$2.00	$15,560
Jun 04	$17.52	$2.00	$15,520
Jul 04	$17.48	$2.00	$15,480
Aug 04	$17.46	$2.00	$15,460
Sep 04	$17.46	$2.00	$15,460
Oct 04	$17.46	$2.00	$15,460
Nov 04	$17.47	$2.00	$15,470
Dec 04	$17.48	$2.00	$15,480

Assuming that the cash flows are received at the end of the month and that the first cash flow will be received at the end of October 2002, the present value, at the end of August 2002, of this stream of certainty equivalent cash flows is $420,411.

12.7)

To compute the risk neutral probabilities of the high and low demand states based on the futures prices and the spot prices expected on the expiration of the futures contract, we use the following formula (from Chapter 7):

$$F = \pi S_u + (1-\pi)S_d \qquad \Rightarrow \qquad \pi = \frac{F-S_d}{S_u - S_d}$$

In this example, since F = $0.60, S_u = $0.90 and S_d = $0.50:

$$\pi = \frac{\$0.60 - \$0.50}{\$0.90 - \$0.50} = \frac{\$0.10}{\$0.40} = 0.25$$

Since the cash flow in the up state is $7,500,000 and the cash flow in the down state is $0 (the mine is shut down), the risk neutral valuation of the mine is:

$$PV_0 = \frac{\pi C_u + (1-\pi)C_d}{1+r_f} = \frac{(0.25 \times \$7,500,000) + (0.75 \times \$0)}{1.05} = \$1,786,000$$

This is the same value found in Example 12.2.

12.8)

a)

The single discount rate will reflect the systematic risk of early-dated cash flows. Hence it will usually be too high with respect to the systematic risk of later-dated cash flows. This would tend to increase the discount rate and yield an underestimation of the NPV of longer-term projects.

b)

Longer-term investment projects tend to embed a larger portfolio of strategic options than shorter-term projects. Hence, strategic options tend to add more value to longer-term projects than to shorter-term ones. Failure to recognize these strategic options and their contributions to the value of longer-term projects will induce managers to prefer, mistakenly, shorter-term projects to longer-term projects, because the later-dated values are underestimated.

12.9)

With a 2 percent interest rate, Micro's balance sheet accounts and expected financial performance for the next year will be as follows:

Assets (book value)	$500,000,000
Liabilities (book value)	$200,000,000
Equity (book and market value)	$300,000,000
Number of shares outstanding	30,000,000
Equity per share (book and market value)	$300,000,000/30,000,000 = $10
Expected net income	$20,000,000 – ($100,000,000)(.02) = $18,000,000
Expected EPS	$18,000,000/30,000,000 = $0.60
P/NI	$10/$0.60 = 16.67

Thus, the Price/Earnings ratio decreases as a result of the increase in leverage. This is because the 5% ratio of unlevered earnings to price exceeds the 2% expected yield on the debt.

12.10)

Building excess capacity may allow a company to deter entry and to maintain market share, thereby keeping product prices from being reduced through competitive entry. The incremental cash flows derived from the excess capacity might then be positive even if the capacity were never used. Furthermore, excess capacity projects may add value by creating the flexibility to satisfy unexpected increases in demand for the product.

12.11)

From equation (12.1):

$$\frac{P}{NI} = \frac{A-D}{X-r_D D} = \frac{1}{r_D}\left\{\frac{\left(A/X\right)Xr_D - r_D D}{X-r_D D}\right\}$$

Rearranging:

$$\frac{P}{NI}(X-r_D D) = \left(A/X\right)X - D \qquad \Rightarrow \qquad A/X = \frac{P/NI(X-r_D D)+D}{X}$$

12.12) [Note: In the first printing of the second edition, the word 'price' is omitted after 'stock' in the first line of this exercise.]

a)

Before the leveraged recapitalization, the dividend per share is $1 and the price per share is $25, so the dividend yield is ($1/$25) = 4.0%. The total amount of the dividends paid is $1 million and the total value of the firm's equity is $25 million, so the dividend yield can also be calculated on an aggregate basis: ($1 million/$25 million) = 4.0%

The company reinvests 50% of its earnings so that, of the $2 million in EBI, $1 million is plowed back in to the firm. Of the remaining $1 million in EBI, (0.06 × $12,500,000) = $750,000 must be used to pay interest if there is a leveraged recapitalization. This leaves $0.25 million to be paid to shareholders. Since there are only half as many shares outstanding after the leverage recapitalization, the dividend yield is ($0.25 million/$12.5 million) = 2.0% after the recapitalization. On a per share basis, the dividend yield is ($0.50/$25) = 2.0%.

b)

From Equation 11.2b:

$$\beta_E = \left(1+\frac{D}{E}\right)\times\beta_A$$

After the leveraged recapitalization, D = E so that:

$$\left(1+\frac{D}{E}\right) = 2$$

Therefore, $\beta_E = 2\times\beta_A$ and the equity risk premium doubles from (10% − 6%) = 4% to 8% so that $\bar{r}_E = 6\% + 8\% = 14\%$

c)

From Equation 9.11: $S_0 = \dfrac{div_1}{\bar{r}_E - g}$

Therefore, solve for g in the following equation: $\$25 = \dfrac{\$0.50}{0.14 - g}$

The solution is: g = 0.12 = 12.0%

CHAPTER 13
CORPORATE TAXES AND THE IMPACT OF FINANCING ON REAL ASSET VALUATION

13.1)

From equation (13.7):

$$\beta_{UA} = \beta_E \Big/ \left[1 + (1 - T_c) \frac{D}{E} \right]$$

For Lockheed, $\beta_{UA,L} = 0.9 / \left[1 + (1 - .34)(0.9) \right] = 0.565$

For Northrop, $\beta_{UA,N} = 0.85 / \left[1 + (1 - .34)(0.7) \right] = 0.581$

13.2)

The β_{UA} of Hughes can be estimated by taking the average of the β_{UA} of the comparison firms:

$$\beta_{UA,H} = \frac{\beta_{UA,L} + \beta_{UA,N}}{2} = \frac{0.565 + 0.581}{2} = 0.573$$

13.3)

The beta of the equity of Hughes can be computed by re-levering the estimated beta of its unlevered assets:

$$\beta_E = \beta_{UA} \left[1 + (1 - T_c) \frac{D}{E} \right]$$

$$\beta_E = 0.573 \left[1.0 + (1.0 - 0.34)(1.0) \right] = 0.95$$

13.4)

Since D/E =1, so that for every $1 of equity there is $1 of debt in the capital structure of the firm, then:

$$w_E = \frac{1}{1+1} = 0.5 \text{ and } w_D = \frac{1}{1+1} = 0.5$$

Then we have:

$$\bar{r}_E = 0.08 + 0.95(0.14 - 0.08) = 0.137 = 13.7\%$$

$$WACC = (0.5)(0.137) + (0.5)(1 - 0.34)(0.08) = 0.095 = 9.5\%$$

13.5)

The value of Hughes can be computed as the present value of an infinite stream of cash flows:

$$PV_0 = \frac{CF_1}{WACC - g} = \frac{\$300\,\text{million}}{0.095 - 0.05} = \$6{,}667\,\text{million}$$

13.6)

For GM, D/E = 0.4 so that for every \$1 of equity there is \$0.40 of debt in the capital structure of the firm, and:

$$w_E = \frac{1}{1+0.4} = 0.714 \quad \text{and} \quad w_D = \frac{0.4}{1+0.4} = 0.286$$

Then we have:

$$\overline{r}_E = 0.08 + (1.2)(0.14 - 0.08) = 0.152 = 15.2\%$$

$$WACC_{GM} = (0.714)(0.152) + (0.286)(1-.34)(0.08) = 0.124 = 12.4\%$$

Then the value of Hughes is:

$$PV_0 = \frac{CF_1}{WACC - g} = \frac{\$300\,\text{million}}{0.124 - 0.05} = \$4{,}054\,\text{million}$$

13.7)

Since $\beta_{UA} = 0.573$:

$$\overline{r}_{UA} = 0.08 + (0.573)(0.14 - 0.08) = 0.1144 = 11.44\%$$

$$PV_0(UA) = \frac{\$300\,\text{million}}{0.1144 - 0.05} = \$4{,}658\,\text{million}$$

Computing the value of the debt tax shield is slightly more complex. Assume that debt is perpetual (i.e., debt is refinanced whenever it matures), and that Hughes wants to maintain a D/E ratio of 1. Since the unlevered cash flows increase by 5% each year, the debt and the debt payments must increase at the same rate in order for D/E to remain constant. This occurs if the interest payment on the debt amounts to 50% of the first year net after tax cash flows (including the tax shield from interest) and then grows at a rate of 5% per year. This implies that rD_1 must satisfy the following equation:

$$rD_1 = (0.50)(\$300\,\text{million} + 0.34rD_1)$$

Solving this equation, we find $rD_1 = \$180.72$ million. The first year tax shield is:

(0.34) (\$180.72 million) = \$61.44 million

These tax shields grow at the same rate as the debt and unlevered cash flow (i.e., 5%). Thus, the PV of the tax shield from interest is:

$$PV_0(\,\text{Interest Tax Shield}\,) = \frac{\$61.44\,\text{million}}{0.08 - 0.05} = \$2{,}048$$

So: APV = \$4,658 + \$2,048 = \$6,706 million

13.8)

a)

$$\beta_E = \left[1 + (1 - T_c)\frac{D}{E}\right]\beta_{UA} = \left[1 + (1 - 0.34)(0.4)\right] \times 0.83 = 1.05$$

b)

$$\overline{r}_E = 0.04 + (1.05)(0.084) = 0.128 = 12.8\%$$

c)

$$WACC = (0.714)(.128) + (0.286)(1 - 0.34)(0.04) = .099 = 9.9\%$$

13.9)

Using the equity betas, leverage proportions of the comparison firms, and equation (13.7), we get:

$$\beta_{UA} = 1.5 \Big/ \left[1 + (1 - 0.5)\frac{0.25}{0.75}\right] = 1.29$$

Now, using the target leverage for GT Widget Company, the equity beta is:

$$\beta_{E,GT} = 1.29\left[1 + (1 - 0.5)\frac{0.60}{0.40}\right] = 2.26$$

The WACC is computed as follows:

$$\overline{r}_E = 0.08 + (2.26)(0.15 - 0.08) = 0.2382 = 23.82\%$$

implying that:

$$WACC = (0.4)(0.2382) + (0.6)(1 - 0.5)(0.14) = 0.137 = 13.7\%$$

13.10)

From the net income data and other data, we reconstruct the after-tax net cash flows of the project. First, we add back the annual depreciation expense which was deducted in the computation of net income, but which is not a cash expense. Second, we add the after-tax salvage value of the machinery. Third, we include the investments and recoveries of net working capital (i.e., the changes in net working capital).

(in $000)	Year	0	1	2	3	4	5
(1)Net Income			$ 40	$ 75	$155	$310	$ 75
(2)Depreciation			100	100	100	100	100
Required NWC		100	200	400	600	200	0
(3)Cash Flow due to NWC		-100	-100	-200	-200	400	200
(4)Capital expenditure		-500					
(5)After-tax proceeds from capital asset sales							60
CF[(1)+(2)+(3)+(4)+(5)]		-$600	$ 40	-$ 25	$ 55	$810	$435

The NPV of the project, discounted at 18%, is $57,350. However, this figure does not take debt tax shields into account.

The tax shields from interest deductibility attributable to this project are the tax shields that arise from the increase in debt capacity provided by the project. Hence only interest on $300,000 for years 1 to 3, and interest on $200,000 for years 4 and 5 is eligible.

Tax shield from interest yr. 1 to 3: ($300,000)(14%)(40%) = $16,800
Tax shield from interest yr. 4 to 5: ($200,000)(14%)(40%) = $11,200
We assume that the tax shields will be used with certainty. Thus the PV of the interest tax shields attributable to the project (using 14% as the discount rate) is $51,452. The APV of the project is:
$57,350 + $51,452 = $108,802

13.11)

If the mold in Example 13.4 is fully equity financed, then:

$$NPV = -\$150,000 + \frac{\$45,000}{1.05} + \frac{\$40,000}{1.05^2} + \frac{\$35,000}{1.05^3} + \frac{\$30,000}{1.05^4} + \frac{\$25,000}{1.05^5} = \$3,642$$

Thus, PV(Debt tax shield) = $11,750 – $3,642 = $8,108.

13.12)

In the up state, the cash flow to existing debt holders is $77 million. In the down state, the cash flow to existing debtholders is:

$103.12 million × (77/(77+31.9)) = $72.9 million

So the risk-neutral discounted value of the existing debt of Unitron is:

$$PV_0 = \frac{(0.5)(\$77 \text{ million}) + (0.5)(\$72.9 \text{ million})}{1.10} = \$68.136 \text{ million}$$

This gives the existing debt holders a gain of $636,000 over the current $67.5 million value of the debt.

13.13)

It makes sense to buy rather than lease if the cost of owning the office space is less than the cost of leasing it. Clearly, it would be inappropriate to use the firm's cost of capital of 20 percent to calculate the cost of owning the building. Since owning the building is assumed to be a risk-free investment and the firm can finance it with a mortgage having a rate equal to the risk-free rate, the after-tax mortgage rate would be [0.08 × (1 – 0.25)] = 6%. The after-tax cost of the mortgage would be (0.06 × $1,000,000) = $60,000 per year. This is about $100,000 per year less than the after-tax lease payments. Hence, the firm is better off if it buys the building rather than leasing it.

The comparison here is equivalent to discounting the $160,000 per year in after-tax lease payments at the 6 percent after-tax discount rate and seeing whether the discounted payments exceed $1,000,000. In this case, the present value of the lease payments in perpetuity is ($160,000/0.06) = $2,666,667, which exceeds the $1,000,000 cost of the cheaper alternative, buying the building. If the firm had used its 20 percent cost of capital to discount the cash flows from the lease payments, the present value of the perpetual lease payments becomes ($160,000/0.20) = $800,000. With the 20 percent cost of capital as the discount rate, AMD would have concluded incorrectly that leasing was the cheaper alternative.

13.14)

If the Modigliani-Miller assumptions hold, the weighted average cost of capital is:

$\bar{r}_E = 0.05 + (1.00)(0.08) = 0.13 = 13\%$

The WACC is 13% regardless of the firm's debt level.

However, if there are taxes, the Modigliani-Miller adjusted cost of capital is:

$$WACC = \bar{r}_{UA}\left[1 - T_c\left(\frac{D}{D+E}\right)\right] = 0.13 \times \left[1 - 0.3\left(\frac{5}{5+1}\right)\right] = .0975 = 9.75\%$$

13.15)

The expected return of Akron's equity is:

$\bar{r}_E = 0.08 + (1.20)(0.13 - 0.08) = 0.14 = 14\%$

The weighted averaged cost of capital is:

$$WACC = w_E\bar{r}_e + w_D(1 - T_c)(\bar{r}_D) = (0.5)(0.14) + (0.5)(1 - 0.4)(0.08) = 0.094 = 9.4\%$$

13.16)

The $25 million reduction in debt reduces the present value of the debt tax shield by:

$T_c \times D = 0.40 \times \$25$ million $= \$10$ million

Thus, after the exchange offer, there is $25 million less debt and ($25 million − $10 million) = $15 million more equity. Therefore:

[D/(D + E)] = ($25 million)/($25 million + $65 million) = 0.278

In order to find the new WACC after the exchange offer, first find $\bar{r}_{UA}$ as follows:

$$WACC = \bar{r}_{UA}\left[1 - T_c\left(\frac{D}{D+E}\right)\right]$$

$$0.094 = \bar{r}_{UA}\left[1 - 0.4\left(\frac{50}{50+50}\right)\right]$$

$$\bar{r}_{UA} = 0.1175$$

Then compute the new WACC:

$$WACC = \bar{r}_{UA}\left[1 - T_c\left(\frac{D}{D+E}\right)\right] = 0.1175 \times [1 - 0.4(0.278)] = .1044 = 10.44\%$$

[Note to instructor: This is a difficult exercise for Chapter 13 because it requires the student to recognize that the value of the equity (and the value of the assets) has decreased by $10 million. Once the student studies Chapter 14, this problem becomes relatively straightforward. Hence we recommend that this exercise either be assigned as part of a combined assignment for Chapter 13 and Chapter 14, or that it be assigned as a challenging problem to motivated students.]

CHAPTER 14
HOW TAXES AFFECT FINANCING CHOICES

14.1)

a)

For the marginal investor, after-tax expected returns for stocks and bonds must be the same, so we solve for T_E in the following equation:

$$r_D (1 - T_D) = \bar{r}_E (1 - T_E)$$

In this case, $T_E = 0.04 = 4.0\%$

b)

For the firm, the after-tax expected cost must be the same for stocks and bonds. Therefore, we solve for p, the probability that the tax shield is utilized, in the following equation:

$$r_D\, p\, (1 - T_c) + (1 - p)\, r_D = \bar{r}_E$$

The solution is: $p = 0.505$

14.2)

Initially, the expected payoff to equity is: $(0.5) \times (\$210 - \$50) + (0.5) \times (\$80 - \$50) = \$95$

Therefore, the price per share is: $\$95/100 = \$0.95$

14.3)

a)

In the good state, both the new debt and the existing debt are paid in full. In the bad state, the debt holders share the available $80 equally because the new debt has the same seniority as the existing debt, and both new and existing debtholders are owed $50. Thus, the new debt has a value of:

$(0.5) \times (\$50) + (0.5) \times (\$40) = \$45$

b)

After the capital structure change, the expected value of the remaining equity is:

$(0.5) \times (\$210 - \$100) + (0.5) \times (\$0) = \$55$

To find out the price per share (s), we must find out how many shares (n) were repurchased at this price. We solve the following two equations:

$ns = \$45$ and $(100 - n)(s) = \$55$

The first equation states that the new debt is used to repurchase shares, and the second states that the value of the shares remaining equals the value of the remaining equity. Solving these equations gives s = $1 and n = 45, which means that the firm uses the proceeds of the new debt to buy back 45 shares at a price of $1 per share.

c)

Without the capital structure change, a shareholder with 20% of the outstanding shares receives the following cash flows:

$$X = \$80 \qquad\qquad X = \$210$$

Initially: $\qquad\quad$ $(20\%) \times (\$80 - \$50) = \$6$ $\qquad\quad$ $(20\%) \times (\$210 - \$50) = \$32$

If the shareholder participates in the refinancing by selling nine shares at $1 per share and using the proceeds to buy $9 of the new debt (which is 1/5 of the new issue), he would be left holding eleven of the 55 remaining shares (which is 1/5 of the remaining equity). In this case, the future cash flows are:

$$X = \$80 \qquad\qquad X = \$210$$

After refinancing: $\qquad$ $(20\%) \times (\$0 + \$40) = \$8$ $\qquad$ $(20\%) \times [(\$50 + (\$210 - \$100)] = \$32$

These cash flows are greater than or equal to the initial cash flows in both states. Thus, the shareholder has improved the future cash flows at no cost today.

d)

Initially, the original debt is riskless and, therefore, has a value of $50. The original total firm value is: ($50 + $95) = $145. After the capital structure change, the value of the old debt decreases to $45. Thus, after the capital structure change, the firm's value is: ($55 + $45 + $45) = $145, the same as before the change.

14.4)

a)

Since the debt is riskless, and both the real and nominal inflation rates are zero, the firm's debt has no interest payments. Since only interest payments are deductible, the firm has no deductions from EBIT.

(in $ millions)	
EBIT	$200.00
Interest deductions	0.00
Taxable income	200.00
Taxes	66.00
Debt payment	50.00
Income for shareholders	$ 84.00

b)

With 10% inflation, EBIT increases by 10%. Also, the firm pays $5 million in deductible interest next year.

(in $ millions)	
EBIT	$220.00
Interest deductions	5.00
Taxable income	215.00
Taxes	70.95
Debt payment	50.00
Income for shareholders	$ 94.05

c)

The income in the inflationary environment is higher, in real terms, by:

($94.05 million/1.10) – $84.00 million = $1.5 million

IGWT gains from the tax shield generated by higher nominal interest payments.

14.5)

In the absence of the refinancing, the investor receives:

$(0.1) \widetilde{X} (1 - 0.34)$

With corporate taxes, the investor receives:

$(0.1)[\widetilde{X} - (\$100 \text{ million}) (0.10)] (1 - 0.34) + (\$10 \text{ million}) (0.08)$

$= (0.1) \widetilde{X} (1 - 0.34) - (\$10 \text{ million}) (0.10)(0.66) + (\$10 \text{ million}) (0.08)$

$= (0.1) \widetilde{X} (1 - 0.34) + \$0.14 \text{ million}$

Therefore, the after tax gain = $0.14 million.

14.6)

An increase in inflation increases the tax gain associated with leverage, since interest rates tend to move in conjunction with inflation. (Indeed, Fisher postulates a one-to-one relation between interest rates and expected inflation.) Thus, inflation affects the capital structure decision by affecting the tax gain from debt; that is, higher inflation implies higher nominal borrowing costs, which creates larger tax deductions.

Inflation affects the capital structure decisions of various firms differently, depending on the ability of the firm to take advantage of its tax shields. For instance, firms with little taxable income may reduce their leverage ratios when inflation increases because inflation increases the magnitude of the tax deduction for each dollar of debt; so less debt is needed to eliminate the firm's tax liability. In contrast, firms with a lot of taxable income may increase their debt ratios since the tax gain from each dollar of debt has increased.

14.7)

Shareholders can buy municipal bonds in order to offset the leverage and tax consequences on their personal portfolios when the firm increases its leverage. (See exercise 14.5.)

14.8)

In the early 1990s, airlines had poor earnings and excess tax shields, effectively placing them in a zero marginal tax bracket. As a result, they could not use the tax benefits associated with leverage. Thus, in order to realize some of the tax benefits, they leased, effectively selling these benefits to tax-paying corporations.

14.9)

    a)

Earnings are not double taxed to the franchise holder. The franchise holder gains from debt only if he can gain by issuing tax-deductible debt and investing the proceeds in municipal bonds.

    b)

In general, the franchise is tax advantaged since the franchise earnings are not double taxed.

14.10)

Since Real Estate Investment Trusts (REITs) do not pay corporate taxes, there are no tax benefits associated with leverage.

14.11)

Inflation increases the debt tax shield and can thus make debt more attractive to some borrowers. This will be the case for Unique Scientific, which is likely to increase its use of debt financing. However, X-Tex Industries, because of other deductions, is able to eliminate its taxes with relatively little debt. X-Tex Industries may reduce its debt level with an increase in inflation because, with inflation, it is able to eliminate its tax liabilities with less debt.

14.12)

The disagreement comes about because Jeff is likely to be subject to high personal taxes and the institutions are tax exempt. From the institutions' perspective, there are substantial tax advantages to increased leverage. However, when Jeff considers how a leverage increase affects his personal taxes, the increase is less attractive.

14.13)

With $10 million of debt at a 10% interest rate, $1 million in pre-tax interest is paid to debt holders. Deducting this $1 million in each of the three scenarios, the expected pre-tax payoff to equity holders is:

(0.3) ($1.5 million $-$ $1 million) $+$ (0.5) ($2 million $-$ $1 million) $+$ (0.2) ($4 million $-$ $1 million)

$=$ $1.25 million

After deducting the 40% corporate tax, the expected payoff is:

$(1 - 0.40)$ ($1.25 million) $=$ $0.75 million

From this $0.75 million, deduct 20% for personal taxes on equity:

$(1 - 0.20)$ ($0.75 million) $=$ $0.60 million

Hence, if debt holders receive $0.60 million in the aggregate, as the equity holders do, then the debt holders' effective personal tax rate on debt is 40%.

14.14)

The value of the tax shield is: $T_g D$

$D = \$100 million$

$$T_g = 1 - \left[\frac{(1 - T_c)(1 - T_E)}{(1 - T_D)} \right] = 1 - \left[\frac{(1 - 0.34)(1 - 0.14)}{(1 - 0.28)} \right] = 0.2117$$

Therefore:

$T_g D = 0.2117 \times \$100 million = \$21.17 million$

CHAPTER 15
HOW TAXES AFFECT DIVIDENDS AND SHARE REPURCHASES

15.1)

The proportion of earnings distributed in the form of a share repurchase has increased substantially over the past 25 years. This cannot be explained by changing tax laws, which have lessened the advantage of repurchases. Perhaps the change is due to a recognition by corporations of academic work preaching the tax advantages of using share repurchases to distribute cash to shareholders, combined with greater incentives to improve shareholder values.

15.2)

Assume that you have no capital gains tax; then the tax rate on dividends (T_E) that will make you indifferent between buying the stock before or after the dividend payment is:

$$98 - 2(1 - T_E) = 96.50$$
$$T_E = 25\%$$

Thus, if your marginal tax rate is greater than 25%, then you prefer to buy the stock after the dividend payment. If $T_E < 25\%$, then you prefer to buy the stock before the dividend payment. Now, if there are also capital gains taxes, the answer depends on how long you intend to hold the stock. If the capital gains tax rate is high and your investment horizon is short, then you might prefer to buy the stock before the dividend payment.

15.3)

No, the Tax Reform Act of 1986 did not eliminate the tax preference for share repurchases over dividends. Investors can defer capital gains indefinitely, thus making the present value of the capital gains tax very small.

15.4)

Since Hot Shot will have substantial tax write-offs initially, it should have little debt in its original capital structure because it cannot realize the tax benefits of leverage. It should then increase leverage by repurchasing shares over time. If it is expected that repurchasing shares will be costly, then the firm might initially include more debt in its capital structure, which would then allow the firm to carry its tax losses forward.

15.5)

A manager wanting to retain as much as possible in the firm would oppose proposals to repurchase shares that would make it less costly to distribute cash to shareholders. Perhaps some managers have been opposed to repurchases for this reason.

15.6)

From equation (15.4), investors prefer retained earnings to cash dividends if:

$(1 - T_c) \times$ (pretax return within corporation) $> (1 - T_E) \times$ (pretax return outside corporation)

(i)   For tax-exempt investors:

$(1 - 0.40) \times (0.08) < (1 - 0) \times (0.08)$

So, tax-exempt investors prefer a dividend.

(ii) For investors with a 25% marginal tax rate:

$(1 - 0.40) \times (0.08) < (1 - 0.25) \times (0.08)$

So, these investors also prefer a dividend.

(iii) For investors with a 40% marginal tax rate:

$(1 - 0.40) \times (0.08) = (1 - 0.40) \times (0.08)$

So, these investors are indifferent.

Consider now the following case: the firm can invest in preferred stock yielding 7% and only 30% of the dividends received are taxed. One can show that, in this case, only the tax-exempt investors prefer the dividends.

15.7)

If the capital gains tax rate is expected to increase, then Bill Gates will likely want to use more of Microsoft's excess cash to repurchase shares now, as they are tax advantaged relative to repurchases of equity in the future when the tax rate increases.

15.8)

a)

Using the dividend discount model from equation (10.5a):

$P_0 = [D_1(1 - T_E)]/(r - g) = \$4(1 - 0.4)/(0.10 - 0.02) = \$30$

b)

Since the effective tax rate on share repurchases is zero:

$P_0 = [D_1(1 - 0)]/(r - g) = \$4/(0.10 - 0.02) = \$50$

15.9)

From Daniel's perspective, the effective tax rate on Alpha's profits is:

$T_c + (1 - T_c)T_E = 0.35 + (1 - 0.35)0.40 = 0.61 = 61\%$

15.10)

The argument would relate to personal taxes as well as corporate taxes. In the initial years, there is no tax advantage associated with a substantial amount of debt financing. However, this situation is likely to change in the future. If the firm is initially financed with a substantial amount of equity, then the firm may want to increase its leverage in the future when the firm's taxable earnings increase. In order to do this, the firm must then either pay out a large dividend or repurchase shares. If Fred would like to eventually reduce his percentage ownership of the firm, a share repurchase would require that he sell more shares and thus realize greater capital gains. A dividend will have a greater impact on his personal taxes.

CHAPTER 16
BANKRUPTCY COSTS AND DEBT HOLDER-EQUITY HOLDER CONFLICTS

16.1)

a)

NPV(A) = (0.5) × ($120 million + $60 million) – $100 million = –$10 million
NPV(B) = (0.5) × ($101 million + $101 million) – $100 million = $1 million

b)

E[equity|A selected] = (0.5) × ($120 million – $100 million + $0 million) = $10 million
E[equity|B selected] = (0.5) × ($101 million – $100 million + $101 million – $100 million)
                     = $1 million

Equity holders prefer project A, a negative NPV project, because debt holders bear most of the downside risk while equity holders receive the upside gain. Thus, equity holders prefer the more risky project. This is an example of asset substitution.

16.2)

a)

All equity firm: (0.5)($210 + $66)(2/3)(1/1.10) = $83.64

b)

Since the debt will be repaid in either state of the economy: D=$44 (1/1.10) =$40

c)

$$E = \frac{(0.5) \times [\$210(2/3) - \$44(0.95)] + (0.5) \times [\$66(2/3) - \$44(0.95)]}{1.10} = \$45.64$$

d)

The firm would be worth ($40.00 + $45.64) = $85.64, so that the debt increases the firm's value.

e)

The firm would be bankrupt if the economy were bad, which would decrease firm value by $20 in the bad state. However, the value of the firm still increases in spite of the bankruptcy cost. To see this:

$$D = \frac{(0.5) \times [\$70 + (\$66 - \$20)]}{1.10} = \$52.73$$

$$E = \frac{(0.5) \times [(\$210)(2/3) - (\$70)(0.95)]}{1.10} = \$33.41$$

Therefore, firm value = ($52.73 +$33.41) = $86.14, which is greater than the $85.64 value computed in part (d).

16.3)

a)

The present values of the three alternatives are:

PV(liq) = $120
PV(A) = (0.5) × ($135+$135) = $135
PV(B) = (0.5) × ($161+$69) = $115

Thus, project A has the highest present value.

b)

Yes, Jack and Jill should agree to loan the firm $20. If they do not make the loan, the firm is liquidated, and they receive nothing. If they make the loan of $20, they will receive $35 if the managers choose project A, and they will receive an expected [0.5 × ($40 + $20.5)] = $30.25 if the managers choose project B. In either case, their $20 investment to save the company from liquidation is a positive NPV investment for them.

c)

The managers, acting in the interests of equity holders, will choose project B. If the firm is liquidated, equity holders receive nothing. If project A is chosen, equity holders also receive nothing because all of the cash flows go to debt payments. If project B is chosen, however, equity holders have a 50% chance of receiving (161 − 100 − 40 − 20.5) > 0. Therefore, equity holders prefer the risky, lower NPV project.

16.4)

a)

NPV[Dress] = (0.3) × ($2 million) + (0.7) × ($9 million) − $6 million = $0.9 million
NPV[Cosmetic] = (0.3) × ($7 million) + (0.7) × ($6 million) − $6 million = $0.3 million

If HFC is all equity financed, then Project Dress is the better project because it has the greater NPV.

b)

If HFC has a $5,000,000 bond obligation at the end of the year, then:

E[equity|Dress] = (0.3)($0 million) + (0.7)($9 million − $5 million) − $6 million + $5 million
= $1.8 million

E[equity|Cosmetic] = (0.3)($7 million − $5 million)
+ (0.7)($6 million − $5 million) − $6 million + $5 million
= $0.3 million.

Therefore, from the stockholders' perspective, even with the $5 million bond obligation, the Project Dress has the higher value

16.5)

NPV(equity) = [(0.9)($153,000) + (0.1)($61,000) − $53,000](.9) − $50,000 = $31,720
NPV(debt) = [(0.9)($153,000 − $53,000)](0.9) − $50,000 = $31,000

Thus, the value of Sigma Design is lower with debt financing since the firm passes up the positive NPV project when the economy is unfavorable.

16.6)

In Japan, financial institutions hold significant equity interests in the borrowing firms; this should reduce the costs of financial distress. The financial institution eliminates much of the debt holder-equity holder conflict since it is essentially both debt holder and equity holder. In other words, any gain typically expropriated by equity holders from debt holders becomes a gain the financial institution also receives. Thus, the financial institution's overall position is less affected by the conflict.

16.7)

The more favorable tax status of equity suggests that the expected returns on corporate bonds should command a premium in order to compensate investors for the relative tax disadvantage. Thus, expected returns on corporate bonds should be higher than expected returns on equity. If interest payments are tax deductible, then there is a tax advantage to debt, and thus the reverse should be true: expected returns on equity should be higher than expected returns on debt. Finally, if bankruptcy costs are important, then firms will not borrow to the point where the after-tax costs of debt and equity are equal. This implies a lower supply of debt in the economy and thus a lower rate of return on the debt.

16.8)

If the firm is all equity financed:

E[NPV$_A$] = (0.5) × ($120 + $90) − $100 = $5
E[NPV$_B$] = (0.5) × ($140 + $60) − $100 = $0

Thus, equity holders prefer project A with the higher expected NPV.

If the firm has an $85 bond obligation due next year:

$E[NPV_A] = (0.5) \times (\$120 - \$85) + (0.5) \times (\$90 - \$85) - \$15 = \$5.00$

$E[NPV_B] = (0.5) \times (\$140 - \$85) + (0.5) \times (\$0) - \$15 = \$12.50$

Thus, equity holders will prefer project B, the project with the lower expected NPV, since the bondholders bear the loss in the bad state.

16.9)

You need to distinguish between a positive NPV project for the firm and a positive NPV project for equity holders. This risk-free project will reduce the value of Tailways' equity since the firm can borrow at 12% while the project yields only 10%. But, debt holders will be better off since the risk-free project will reduce the overall riskiness of the firm's debt, increasing the value of that debt. Thus, the total value of the firm will increase. This must be the case since a riskless project yielding a return greater than the risk-free rate is an arbitrage opportunity, when combined with appropriately designed financing in the financial markets, and thus must create value for the firm.

16.10)

Equity holders prefer risky projects since equity holders essentially own an option on the value of the firm's assets. In addition, equity holders are less likely to liquidate since this will effectively terminate the option, and they will attempt to keep the firm's operations going in order to maintain a positive probability of having a high payoff in the future. Debt holders, on the other hand, prefer safe projects, and are likely to liquidate the firm, especially if they will receive payment on most of their claims through the liquidation.

16.11)

Debt holder-equity holder incentive problems are less severe for firms that borrow short-term because the value of short-term debt is much less sensitive to changes in a firm's investment strategy. Also, short-term debt makes it more difficult for equity holders to gain at the expense of debt holders by choosing riskier projects.

16.12)

The NPV is: $[(0.20) \times (\$85 \text{ million}) + (0.80) \times (\$150 \text{ million})] - \$75 \text{ million} = \$62 \text{ million}$

The firm cannot issue equity to fund the project because equity holders will not be willing to finance the project. Equity holders will not be willing to finance the project because the value of the equity $[(0.20)(\$85 \text{ million}) + (0.80)(\$150 \text{ million}) - \$70 \text{ million} = \$67 \text{ million}]$ is less than the project cost ($75 million).

16.13)

The firm can issue equity to fund the more capital-intensive project since the value of the equity $[(0.80)(\$170 \text{ million} - \$70 \text{ million}) = \$80 \text{ million}]$ is greater than the project cost ($75 million). In the bad state of the economy, the firm would be unable to meet its bond obligation and would be bankrupt.

16.14)

The existing debt holders can benefit from DIP financing because the weakening of their seniority allows the firm to make good investments (i.e., it eliminates the debt overhang problem). In equilibrium, this will be true if DIP financing can only be obtained in extreme situations, that is, when the firm has promising and profitable projects that will increase firm value, rather than projects designed to expropriate wealth from debt holders to equity holders. Consequently, DIP financing must impose a cost on firms so that high quality firms (those with projects that increase firm value) can credibly signal their intention to invest in good projects. Using the costly process of obtaining DIP financing provides such a signal.

16.15)

Now that Emax Industries has become more flexible, it can change its investment strategy more quickly, enabling it to invest in riskier projects or to pursue other strategies that transfer wealth from debt holders to equity holders more quickly. Thus, the value of Emax Industries bonds is likely to decline.

16.16)

Since Atways Industries can default on the Montana project without going bankrupt, the Montana project is more likely to be subject to equity holder-debt holder conflicts. Specifically, the incentive to increase risk is likely to be greater for the Montana project. If the borrowing rate on the Montana project is higher than the corporation's borrowing rate, then the underinvestment problem is also likely to be greater for the Montana project.

CHAPTER 17
CAPITAL STRUCTURE AND CORPORATE STRATEGY

17.1)

Direct bankruptcy costs include legal fees associated with bankruptcy proceedings, costs of liquidation (i.e., the tendency for debt holders to favor liquidation, which may be sub-optimal), and the time management spends on bankruptcy issues. Indirect costs include the tendency for suppliers, customers and employees to demand added compensation or terms less favorable to the firm when dealing with a firm in financial distress. The majority of these costs are borne by the debt holders and the non-financial stakeholders of the firm, but some of these costs are also passed on to equity holders.

17.2)

As a potential employee, you might be interested in the firm's capital structure because a firm that carries a large amount of debt has a high probability of default; consequently, you may be concerned about the longevity and career opportunities of your employment. If the firm goes bankrupt, you could lose your job, but even if the firm does not enter bankruptcy, you may be concerned that it is in financial distress. If in financial distress, the firm may limit opportunities for its employees and may have difficulty meeting compensation packages and bonuses. In addition, your bargaining power is lessened in a financially distressed firm since you will be deterred from pushing the firm into bankruptcy.

17.3)

A high-tech start-up computer firm must provide maintenance, product support, and a high quality product, and must have cash on hand, solid and reliable suppliers, specialized human capital, and the ability to react quickly to market conditions. A firm of this type in financial distress would find it difficult to maintain these conditions. All of these characteristics make the financial distress conditions very costly for the firm; thus, the indirect costs of bankruptcy are very high. Conversely, a hotel chain requires little cash, and has very observable product quality and unspecialized labor. Thus, the indirect bankruptcy costs for hotels are relatively small.

17.4)

The firm is currently paying 10%, or $10 million, in interest each year, leaving only $10 million ($20 million – $10 million) of operating income. If the union wants a wage increase from $20 to $25 per hour, the total increased cost to the firm is:

($5) × (1000 workers) × (2000 hours/worker) = $10 million

This will eliminate the remaining profit. So, if the firm increases its debt to $150 million, the union's request would push the firm into bankruptcy. With this higher debt ratio, the union will have to settle for less than $22.50 per hour.

17.5)

Since the expected value of the repurchase is $48 million, and the cost imposed by the suppliers is $30 million (2% × $1.5 billion), BCD should repurchase 40% of its common stock.

17.6)

If the manager of Lung Decay expects that Carcinogens-R-Us will be forced to liquidate or lose market share, then the manager would reduce prices in order to gain market share and send Carcinogens-R-Us into bankruptcy. If, on the other hand, the manager expects its competitor to emerge with no harm, then the manager would maintain prices at current levels, so as to avoid losing profitability without gaining a competitive advantage.

17.7)

Apple has very little debt in its capital structure because: Apple has a highly specialized labor force, product quality for Apple is important and difficult to observe, and its line of business requires future servicing and support. All of these factors make the indirect costs of financial distress large. Marriott, on the other hand, has: very little specialized labor, observable product quality, and little additional product support. Thus, Marriott's relatively low indirect costs of financial distress allow it to use a fairly large amount of debt.

17.8)

The costs and benefits of raising prices are: the firm might lose market share, but profits might increase in the short run. Interest rates affect this decision because higher rates decrease the present value of the future benefits associated with higher market share. Thus, if one considers lowering prices in order to achieve greater market share in the future, by sacrificing profitability today, this decision might depend on the level of interest rates. If rates are high, then the future benefits are discounted more heavily, and thus the firm may prefer to increase profitability today in lieu of increasing future market share.

17.9)

At a borrowing rate of 16%, the net present value from laying off the workers is:

$50 million − ($70 million/1.16^3) = $5.2 million

The positive NPV indicates a gain associated with laying off workers.

At a borrowing rate of 11%, the NPV is −$1.2 million. At this rate, Weston should not lay off its workers.

If Weston increases its leverage, then a prospective employee will be less likely to work at Weston because the probability of being laid off has increased.

17.10)

Compass may choose not to issue equity to solve its financial problems because issuing equity transfers wealth from existing shareholders to existing debt holders, and may also reduce the bargaining power the firm has with its employees and suppliers. If Compass does not issue equity, then perhaps it should change its product market strategy, particularly if this improves its relationships with its non-financial stakeholders and reduces its vulnerability to competitors.

17.11)

You would rather your competitor have high leverage, because high leverage makes a firm less flexible and increases the probability of financial distress. As a result, the competitor would be more likely to cut corners, and to have poor relations with customers, suppliers, and employees. The more highly levered competitor may also be less aggressive in stealing market share; although this is not always the case.

17.12)

Compton needs a cash inflow of $10 million. If Compton obtains the $10 million through an equity offering, the value of the firm would increase by $10 million. However, the value of the bonds would also increase because the probability of default would decrease. The bonds are currently selling for $30 million ($50 million × 0.6), so a 20% increase would result in a value of $36 million. Thus, the increase in the value of the equity is only $4 million ($10 million – $6 million). Hence investors would not be willing to invest an additional $10 million dollars in equity.

17.13)

a)

If the firm finances the acquisition with equity, then Michael Dell's percentage stake in the company will be reduced. If he would like to reduce his stake, this allows him to do so without selling shares and having to pay a capital gains tax.

b)
If Dell is selling a product that only Dell can service, then financial distress costs are likely to be high, which makes debt less attractive.

c)
If Dell is likely to be generating excess cash in the future, it will be able to quickly pay down the debt from internal funds. Without debt, the alternative is to pay the money out as a dividend or to repurchase shares, which could have adverse tax implications for Dell's shareholders.

17.14)

Chrysler management argued that the cash was needed in order to absorb losses in the event of a recession. Management argued that Chrysler needed to lock in long term debt in good times, because, in the event of a recession, Chrysler would not be able to borrow.

17.15)

When grocery stores lower prices, they generally make less money in the short-run, but they attract more customers, which allows them to make more money in the long run. Hence, their incentive to price aggressively is likely to be determined by the rate at which they discount future cash flows. Following leveraged buyouts, firms have high cost debt obligations that they have an incentive to pay down quickly. Hence, they are less willing to take actions, like lowering prices, that are costly in the short run but have long run benefits.

17.16)

With lower transaction costs we might expect firms to more aggressively use debt financing. Financial distress is likely to be less costly if the firm can easily issue new equity and use the proceeds to pay down debt. However, there is no empirical evidence that suggests that firms are taking advantage of lower transaction costs in this way.

CHAPTER 18
HOW MANAGERIAL INCENTIVES AFFECT FINANCIAL DECISIONS

18.1)

There are two reasons that managers want their organizations to grow. First, a growing organization can reduce the probability of bankruptcy and financial distress. This can increase managers' job security and it can also allow managers to reward their employees. Second, the larger the size of the firm, the more the firm can increase the financial and non-financial compensation of the manager.

18.2)

Ownership concentration is determined primarily by two factors: (1) a firm's size or its development stage, and (2) the type of firm or the kind of assets it owns

A firm that generates large control benefits usually has higher ownership concentration. For example, in the entertainment and media industries, owners do not want to give up ownership because they can enjoy the numerous non-financial benefits associated with control of these industries.

Firms with a lot of intangible assets usually have greater agency problems and thus higher ownership concentration in order to mitigate these problems.

A firm that is smaller or in an early stage of development generally has an owner or entrepreneur with a higher ownership percentage.

18.3)

In the first scenario, the CEO will own approximately (25/75) = 1/3 of the firm and may therefore lose some control. There might then be an offsetting impact on his incentives. Under the alternative scenario, the CEO of High Tech retains 51% of the firm and thus indirectly controls the subsidiary as well. However, since his indirect ownership of the subsidiary is less than his ownership of the parent, he will have an incentive to transfer resources from the subsidiary to the parent. It will be easier to motivate the manager of Super Tech if Super Tech has its own publicly traded stock.

18.4)

Firm 1 generally has the optimal ratio of debt as described in this text. Firm 2 generally has a higher debt ratio since the board wants to reduce the manager's investment flexibility. Firm 3 is expected to have a lower debt ratio since the manager prefers maximum investment flexibility and wishes to minimize bankruptcy risk.

18.5)

If it is more difficult to extract private benefits from partial control over management, large shareholders will own fewer shares and monitor less. Because of the free-rider problem, there will be too little monitoring in the absence of these private benefits. To solve the free-rider problem, the level of private benefits should just compensate shareholders for the social benefits they create by monitoring.

18.6)

It is much easier to base compensation for the Chevron CEO on relative performance. The Chevron CEO can be judged by how well the firm has done relative to changes in the price of oil and relative to its competitors. Using relative performance to compensate the CEO of Chrysler would be more difficult. The auto industry is more concentrated, implying that the CEO's decisions affect the value of Chrysler's competitors. If auto company CEOs all had relative performance compensation packages, they would compete more aggressively which would make the industry less profitable. This would not be as big a problem in the oil industry, which is already very competitive.

18.7)

Firms with higher market-to-book ratios generally have more intangible assets and, hence, there is more scope for the CEO to take actions that benefit him personally, at the expense of the firm. Therefore, stock-based compensation is needed to align the executives' incentives. One might also posit that the causation is reversed. Firms with more stock-based performance have higher market-to-book ratios because they are better managed and thus achieve higher market values.

18.8)

Managers will hold a larger percent of the shares, thus making their incentives more aligned with shareholder value. In addition, bankruptcy is more likely following the transaction, giving the managers a smaller margin for error. For these reasons, the firm's managers are less likely to choose negative NPV investments that benefit them personally.

Because of the higher leverage, the managers may have an incentive to increase risk in order to benefit shareholders (and their own shares) at the expense of debt holders. However, if the managers are very risk averse, they may actually be less likely to take on more risk because they will personally find bankruptcy costly.

Given the high borrowing costs, the firm is likely to choose projects that pay off very quickly.

18.9)

The Chicago Bulls coach can be rewarded based on the success of his team or based on the quality of his decisions. If the team's success were completely under the coach's control, then it would make sense to base the coach's bonus solely on the Bull's winning percentage. However, veteran players get injured, rookies turn out to be either much better or much worse than anticipated, and numerous other factors beyond the coach's control affect winning percentages. In summary, great coaches can be unlucky and therefore fail to deliver a winning season.

One alternative is to reward the coach on the basis of the quality of his decisions. In theory this can be done; however, in reality, an evaluation of this type is likely to be very subjective and may not provide an accurate assessment of the quality of his coaching.

In reality, we expect that a combination of the approaches should be used.

CHAPTER 19
THE INFORMATION CONVEYED BY FINANCIAL DECISIONS

19.1)

If management is highly concerned about the firm's current stock price, the manager would forgo a positive NPV project if financing the project required an equity issue, as this would reduce the price of the stock. Management might also prefer projects with lower NPVs, which pay off sooner, to higher NPV projects that pay off over a longer time period.

19.2)

Increasing the debt level can serve as a signal to the market that the firm has favorable future prospects. Since debt reduces managers' flexibility and increases the probability of financial distress or bankruptcy, only firms with good prospects are willing to take on the extra risk and costs. Managers signal good prospects by increasing debt because the benefits exceed the costs. If this is so, the signal is credible.

19.3)

There are two possible explanations for the fact that stock prices generally respond more negatively to stock issuance announcements by industrial firms than to announcements by utilities. The first is that utilities issue equity on a more regular basis and, as a result, the announcements come as less of a surprise. The second is that utilities are probably subject to less asymmetric information, implying that an equity issuance is less likely to be viewed as a signal that utilities are undervalued.

19.4)

There are a number of reasons why firms tend to invest more when they have more cash available.

Because of personal taxes (see Chapter 15), it may make sense to invest internally generated cash in marginal projects rather than pay out the cash to shareholders. One can make the same argument if there are transaction costs associated with raising or paying out capital.

As discussed in Chapter 18, self-interested managers may have an incentive to invest internally generated cash on marginal projects that benefit the managers personally.

Firms that do not have sufficient cash may pass up positive NPV projects that they would otherwise fund. This could be because of the underinvestment/debt overhang problem (see Chapter 16), or because managers are reluctant to issue equity for information reasons, as discussed in this chapter.

Because managers have superior information relative to outside investors, the manager can take advantage of his superior knowledge by issuing equity when the stock is overvalued. Outside investors, knowing this, would take equity issues as a negative signal and discount the stock price accordingly. As a result, firms may pass up good projects when they cannot finance them either with cash on hand or by borrowing.

19.5)

A manager close to retirement puts more weight on the current stock price than does a manager far from retirement. By selecting a higher debt ratio, the manager signals a higher current stock price (temporarily) which benefits him either in the form of a 'glory' retirement or a higher stock price if he sells his holdings of the company. This increased incentive to signal implies that the manager closer to retirement needs more debt to signal the firm's higher value.

19.6)

Price with the new project: $620/100=$6.20

To finance the project, ABC must issue $100/$6.20=16.1 new shares.

Subsequent price if ABC finances the new investment:

($1000 + $120)/(100+16.1) = $9.65

Subsequent price if ABC passes up the new investment:

$1000/100 = $10.00

If management wants to maximize the intrinsic value of ABC's shares, they should pass up the new investment.

19.7)

When the quality of information improves, it becomes easier for firms to issue outside equity as well as long-term debt. This is because increased quality of disclosures generally makes it more difficult for insiders to take actions that expropriate value from outside shareholders and bondholders. Given this, greater disclosure leads to reductions in equity held by insiders and a greater use of long-term debt financing.

19.8)

Managers might sell shares because of portfolio diversification considerations, but the market may interpret such activity as a signal that managers are pessimistic about the firm's future prospects. Increasing leverage generally indicates that managers are confident about the future earnings and performance of the firm. If the two actions occur simultaneously, the former can reduce the credibility of the signal indicated by the latter. In general, signals are less credible if managers are seen to have a strong interest in temporarily increasing the firm's stock price. This will be the case when: the manager plans to sell stock; the manager has stock-based compensation; or, the firm is a takeover target.

19.9)

State of the Economy	Low	Cash Flows Average.	High
Management's beliefs	$400	$500	$600
Analysts' beliefs	$300	$400	$500
Cost of distress	$100	$150	$200

The intrinsic value is higher if the firm does not incur any cost of financial distress; this is the case if the debt payments are less than $400. If management places equal weight on intrinsic value and current value, then management has to take on interest payments up to $500. The reason is that, even if the analysts are correct about future cash flows, the manager has the incentive to take on debt of $400 to boost the current stock price, while sacrificing some of the intrinsic value of the firm through greater financial distress costs.

19.10)

	State:	Value	
		Low	High
Cash		$100	$100
Fixed asset value		$200	$300
Growth opportunity NPV		$100	$100

The answer depends on investors' beliefs. Assume that investors believe that the firm issues equity only when the firm's fixed assets equal $200. We will show that these beliefs are self-fulfilling.

If the firm is in the high state:

Do nothing:
value of original equity = $100 + $300 = $400
Issue riskless debt to finance the project:
value of original equity = $100 + $300 + $100 = $500
[Since I = $200 < ($100 + $200), the debt is riskless in both states]
Issue equity:
value of original equity = ($300/$400) × $600 = $450

Therefore, the firm prefers to finance the project with debt. If it can not issue debt, the firm is better off issuing equity and taking the project.

19.11)

Since Mr. Smith cares more about intrinsic value while Mr. Chan cares more about current stock price, Mr. Smith's announcement is more credible. Therefore, Mr. Smith's firm should expect the greater stock price increase.

19.12)

Since the warrants are a bet against the firm, the outside investor should become less optimistic about Hopewell's future profits. Warrants are more valuable when volatility is higher; therefore, the incentive to issue warrants is higher when volatility is expected to be low.

19.13)

Increasing leverage with exchange offers signals to the market that management is confident about the future performance of the firm. Consequently, stock prices generally increase.

19.14)

a. If the firm is fairly valued, management should probably issue equity since this is a risky business and, for the reasons discussed in Chapter 17, the firm requires a relatively low debt ratio in order to sell its high-tech farm equipment.

b. If the firm is slightly undervalued, management may choose to issue convertible bonds. As mentioned in (a), the firm has an incentive to issue equity, but may choose to avoid doing so if its equity is sufficiently underpriced. Convertible debt is also underpriced in this situation, but not as much as the firm's equity.

c. If the firm's equity is substantially undervalued, its convertible debt will also be undervalued. To avoid the dilution costs associated with selling an undervalued security, the firm may choose to take out a bank loan. However, this is a risky strategy; if the firm does poorly, and therefore has difficulty meeting its debt obligations, the firm's ability to attract new customers will deteriorate which will in turn worsen the firm's financial situation.

19.15)

The stock price increase does not necessarily indicate that the market viewed the dividend increase as a good decision. The direct impact of a dividend increase may decrease the after-tax returns to shareholders. But the information content of a dividend increase may reveal favorable information about the firm's future cash flows.

19.16)

Since managers are usually replaced following a hostile takeover, management wants to reduce the probability of a hostile takeover. If the probability of a hostile takeover decreases as the firm's share price increases, management is more willing to take short-sighted actions that temporarily increase share price when there is a threat of hostile takeover.

19.17)

Since default wold occur in two of the three demand scenarios, a debt obligation above $400 million will result in a gain in firm value of only [$50 million – (2/3)$60 million] = $10 million. As shown in Example 19.7, the firm obtains a higher value with less than $400 million in debt.

CHAPTER 20
MERGERS AND ACQUISITIONS

20.1)

The 10% increase in earnings should increase the firm's value by 10%, to $27.5 million. Since the cost-savings are risk free, they are discounted at the risk-free rate:

$[\$700,000/.05] \times [1 - (1/1.05)^{10}] = \$5,405,214.45 \approx \$5.4$ million.

Therefore, after the LBO, the value of Jacobs Industries is about $32.9 million, compared to $25 million before the LBO.

20.2)

Following the LBO, John Jacobs' incentives have changed. It is likely that his percentage ownership of the firm has changed. Previously, he may have owned a small percentage of the firm, so he may have been motivated towards managerial perks and negative NPV projects that increase the size of the firm, rather than creating shareholder value. He also may have been motivated to expend resources in order to signal that the firm has a high value. After the LBO, his incentives are likely to change so that he is more concerned with maximizing the intrinsic value of the firm.

20.3)

A diversified firm may be less likely to experience financial distress than a focused firm would be. However, it may be more difficult to track management performance and to create performance incentives in a diversified firm. If managerial performance is worse in the diversified firm, the salaries are likely to be lower in order to adjust for the reduced overall performance and effort.

20.4)

It does not necessarily imply that Cigmatics is a bad acquisition. The decision may be a good one, but the stock market may be reacting to the acquisition offer's signal about the value of Diversified rather than the value of the Cigmatics acquisition. For example, the decision to exchange shares may signal to the market that Diversified management believes that its stock is overvalued.

20.5)

Firms with stable cash flows and unspecialized products have relatively more certain future cash flows and lower financial distress costs, thus making it easier to borrow and to increase leverage. Moreover, these firms generally have high taxable incomes, so higher leverage increases the debt tax shield, generating another source of incremental value.

20.6)

If managers are rewarded for increases in earnings per share, we would expect to see acquisitions that are motivated by increases in EPS. A takeover should be initiated when synergies or other value increasing effects exist. If a takeover increases earnings per share but destroys value, then it does not benefit shareholders.

20.7)

A food company may be worth less when merged with a tobacco company because the food company may have to bear some of the costs associated with the product liability lawsuits. There is a cost associated with providing plaintiff lawyers more assets to go after. However, tobacco companies can gain the flexibility of being able to switch resources from tobacco to food in the event that they are forced to scale back their tobacco business.

20.8)

Even if top management does not change following a buyout, the incentives of the managers may be realigned following a buyout. After a buyout, free cash flow decreases and top managers' ownership in the firm increases; both of these factors help to realign management's incentives with those of the shareholders.

20.9)

AT&T may prefer higher reported earnings if creditors base their covenants and borrowing rates on earnings. Thus, if AT&T could get pooling of interest accounting treatment for its acquisition of NCR, it could increase reported earnings and improve its borrowing terms with creditors. The imposed borrowing terms and other benefits from higher earnings offset the $500 million cost. The top managers of AT&T might also be evaluated and compensated based on reported earnings.

CHAPTER 21
RISK MANAGEMENT AND CORPORATE STRATEGY

21.1)

Small firms hedge less because the fixed costs of hedging are large. Hedging requires a level of knowledge, skill, and sophistication among a firm's employees that small firms generally do not have. The large economies of scale make it more costly for small firms to hedge. If the fixed cost of hedging declines in the future, and employees acquire the required skills, then small firms will hedge more in the future.

21.2)

Managers want to hedge real changes in foreign exchange rates. Unfortunately, it is generally possible to hedge only nominal changes in foreign exchange rates. When inflation rates are volatile, one might actually increase risk while trying to hedge real exchange rate changes with nominal forward and futures contracts.

21.3)

The resort is exposed to US$/CAN$ exchange rate risk. Many U.S. and Canadian skiers will visit the resort if the US$ is high relative to the CAN$, and will ski in the U.S. if it is low. Moreover, if the US$ is high relative to European currencies, U.S. skiers may prefer European skiing. So the resort is also likely to be exposed to European currency exchange rates.

21.4)

Optimal debt levels should rise. Risk management allows firms to reduce the probability of bankruptcy and financial distress. As more firms are able to manage much of their risk exposure, they are able to take on higher debt levels.

21.5)

It is more difficult to hedge the risk in Turkey because of the high inflation rate volatility that results from uncertain monetary policy. (See exercise 21.2.)

21.6)

If PPP holds, many firms do not need to hedge their long-term foreign exchange exposure because nominal price level changes will perfectly offset the fluctuation in nominal exchange rates. For example, changes in Turkish labor costs will remain constant in U.S. dollars if PPP between the U.S. and Turkey remains constant. Hence, U.S. manufacturers in Turkey may not have to hedge against changes in the Turkish lira.

21.7)

Oil firms should hedge part of their exposure to oil price movements in order to reduce the probability of financial distress. However, they want to leave the upside open so that they can reap the benefit of upward price movement. Since exploration expenses are generally higher when oil prices are high, leaving the upside open can generate higher profit to cover the increased expense and to enable more favorable borrowing terms when investment needs are high.

21.8)

The firm can roll over short-term loans and enter into an interest rate swap at the same time.

Borrow short term: $i_{st} = r_{st} + d_{st}$

Swap the interest rate r_{st} for r_l so that:

total rate: $i_{st} = r_l + d_{st}$

Now the firm is not exposed to interest rate movements, but it can benefit from an improvement in its credit rating as d_{st} decreases over the next two years.

CHAPTER 22
THE PRACTICE OF HEDGING

22.1)

National Petroleum can buy put options in order to create a floor for its profits. With the puts, National Petroleum can lock in a profit of [($20 – $6 – $2) × 1 million] = $12 million in year 1, and also earn profits if oil prices exceed $20/barrel. Similarly, the firm can lock in profits of $11 million in year 2 and $10.5 million in year 3.

By hedging in this way, the firm eliminates the possibility of financial distress. By structuring its hedge in this way, National Petroleum will have more money available when oil prices are high and the firm requires new capital. However, National Petroleum is still likely to require access to outside capital in this case.

22.2)

a)

The relative magnitude of the futures and forward prices for copper should be 1. (The futures and forward prices are generally the same for valuation.)

Let r = risk-free rate, y = convenience yield, t = years to forward or futures maturity,

S_0 = spot price of copper

$$F_0 = S_0 (1 + r)^t (1 + y)^{-t} = S_0 \left(\frac{1 + r}{1 + y} \right)^t$$

Since $r > y$, the futures (and forward) price increases with t. The rate of increase is approximately 2% per year.

If the rates are continuously compounded: $F_0 = S_0\, e^{(r-y)t}$

Throughout the rest of this problem, we assume rates are continuously compounded.

b)

To hedge the obligation to buy 1 million pounds of copper three years from now by selling forward contracts to buy copper one year from now, sell $e^{-2y} = e^{-2 \times .03} = 0.9418$ million pounds in forwards now.

At the end of the first year, the hedge ratio changes to: $e^{-y} = e^{-.03} = 0.9704$

At the end of the second year, the ratio is 1.

The intuition is that the position to buy the copper three years hence has the least risk because it has the greatest convenience value. To avoid over-hedging, the ratio should be less than one when the maturities do not match.

c)

We have to tail futures in light of the mark-to-market cash flow feature. This feature makes the futures contract more risky than the forward contract, so the hedge ratio should be further reduced.

For a three-month futures, the hedge ratio is:

$$\frac{\dfrac{1}{e^{3y}}}{\dfrac{1}{e^{0.25y}}\,e^{0.25r}} = \frac{1}{e^{2.75y+0.25r}} = \frac{1}{e^{2.75\times.03+0.25\times.05}} = 0.9094$$

The hedge ratio also increases over time as the futures contract approaches maturity. The hedge ratio approaches the forward hedge ratio:

$$\frac{1}{e^{2.75\times.03}} = 0.9208$$

Immediately after the first futures contract expires at the end of the third month, the hedge ratio with a new futures contract becomes:

$$\frac{1}{e^{2.5\times.03+0.25\times.05}} = 0.9162$$

Let n stand for the nth adjustment of the rollover strategy. Then the hedge ratio is:

$$\frac{1}{e^{(3-0.25n)y+0.25r}}$$

As n approaches 12, the hedge ratio goes to $e^{-0.25\times.05} = 0.9876$, and then gradually increases to one as this futures contract approaches maturity.

22.3)

To reduce its exposure by half, ExxonMobil must solve the following two equations:

$10 million + $10,000 X_{OIL} = $5 million

$20 million + $100,000 $X_{\$/\epsilon}$ = $10 million

The solution is: $X_{OIL} = -500$ and $X_{\$/\epsilon} = -100$

To reduce its exposure, Exxon can short 500 futures contracts for the oil price risk and short 100 futures for the exchange rate risk.

22.4)

	Advantages	Disadvantages
Forwards	Complete hedge if the deal is consummated.	No flexibility. If the deal is not consummated, the hedge creates an exposure.
Options	Creates a cap for the dollar cost of the deal whether or not the deal is consummated.	Options cost money.
Swap	GM can generate (borrow) US$ in US and swap for ¥, creating a ¥ outflow without incurring much foreign exchange risk.	Same as forwards. However, typically, swaps generate a stream of payments. GM needs a one-time customized swap in this case, which may generate larger transaction costs than a forward.

22.5)

Schering-Plough can use swaps to create a synthetic foreign cash flow to cover the foreign liabilities. Suppose 10% euro bonds swap for 7% US$ bonds in the currency swap market and that the current exchange rate is €5/US$. Then:

Cash outflow (euro liabilities) from operations:

Year:	1	2	3	. . .	10
outflows (euros)	100 million	100 million	100 million	. . .	1100 million

Cash flows from 10-year currency swap with 1000 million euros notional amount

Year:	1	2	3	. . .	10
Inflows (euros)	100 million	100 million	100 million	. . .	1100 million
Outflows ($)	14 million	14 million	14 million	. . .	214 million

Net cash flows are then equivalent to that of a $200 million, 7% straight annual-paying coupon bond in US dollars, with a maturity of 10 years.

22.6)

a)

For every one unit increase in the $/€ 1-year forward exchange rate, Dell's European profits increase by $8 million. If the operation is not scalable, then Dell should short 1-year forward contracts on € 8 million. If the operation is scalable, then the answer might change if we hold the total capital expenditure constant.

The standard deviation of $/€ exchange rate is 10%. Profit at risk at the 5% significance level is: $1.65 \times \$8$ million $\times 0.10 = \$1.32$ million.

22.7)

a)

CF
- 0.5 → £5 million
- 0.5 → £2 million

$$F_0 = S_0 \left(\frac{1+r_\$}{1+r_£}\right)' = 1.55 \left(\frac{1.065}{1.117}\right)^{\frac{10}{12}} = 1.4896 \text{ \$/£}$$

Since 1.60 is greater than 1.4896, the highest dollar amount you can lock in today is:

$1.60 \times £2$ million = $3.2 million

Additional forward hedging up to £5 million does not affect variability overall, but it transfers variability from the up state to the down state. Thus, the firm may simply want to hedge £2 million with a forward contract. The remaining unhedged £3 million in the up state may be better hedged (in part or in total) with an option, the cost of which reduces the cash flow in the down state, but by a known (and possibly small) amount. This might be desirable if there are significant financial distress costs, which would preclude overhedging in the down state with forwards, even though such additional hedging with forwards reduces risk in the up state.

b)

There is an arbitrage opportunity. For example:

1) Borrow $1 today, convert it to £ at the current spot rate: $1/1.55 = £0.6452$

2) Lend £ 0.6452 out for 10 months and receive: $[0.6452\,(1+.117)^{10/12}] = £0.7075$

3) Convert it back at the forward rate: $\$1.60(£0.7075) = \$1.1320$

4) Pay the interest and principal of: $(1+.065)^{10/12} = 1.0539$

Retain the arbitrage profit of ($1.1320 − $1.0539) = $0.0781 from the transaction.

22.8)

$S_0 = \$20/\text{barrel}$, $r = 10\%$

Position	Position value $S_0 = \$20$	Position value $S_0 = \$21$ $F=\$20\times1.10=\$22$	Mark-to-market cash $F=\$21\times1.10=\$23.1$	Net gain from the position
Long 1 barrel of oil	$20	$21	$0	$1
a) Sell 1 forward (which offsets the long oil position's net gain)	$0	($22/1.10)−$21=−$1	$0	−$1
b) Sell (1/1.10) futures (which offsets the long oil position's net gain)	$0	$0	−$1	−$1

c)

Position	Position value $S_o = \$20$	Position value $S_o = \$21$ $F = \$22$	Mark-to-market Cash $F = \$23.1$	Net gain from the position
Short 5000 barrels of oil	$-\$20 \times (5000) =$ $-\$100,000$	$-\$105,000$	$\$0$	$-\$5000$
Long 5000 forwards	$\$0$	$5000 \times (\$21 - \$22/1.10)$ $= \$5000$	$\$0$	$\$5000$
Long $(5000/1.10)$ futures	$\$0$	$\$0$	$(\$5000/1.10)(1.10)$ $= \$5000$	$\$5000$

22.9)

a)

Initially the hedge ratio $= 1.02^{-1/2} = 0.9901$, so buy forwards to purchase $(1.5 \text{ million} \times 0.9901) = 1.4852$ million barrels of oil.

At the end of the first three months, the hedge ratio is $1.02^{-1/4} = 0.9951$, so buy forwards to purchase $(1.5 \text{ million} \times 0.9951) = 1.4927$ million barrels of oil.

At the end of the second three months, the hedge ratio is 1, so buy forwards to purchase 1.5 million barrels of oil.

b)

For futures, we need to adjust for the interest received on the cash exchanged due to marking to market:

$$\text{hedge ratio} = \frac{1}{(1+y)^{1/2}(1+r)^{1/4}} = \frac{1}{(1+.02)^{1/2}(1+.09)^{1/4}} = 0.9690.$$

This hedge ratio increases over time as the exponent of 1.09 decreases. Immediately after the first futures contract expires, the new hedge ratio becomes:

$$(1+.02)^{-1/4}(1+.09)^{-1/4} = 0.9739.$$

This hedge ratio also increases over time. Immediately after the second futures contract expires, the new hedge ratio becomes:

$$(1+.09)^{-1/4} = 0.9787$$

Over time, this hedge ratio increases towards one.

c)

If EXCO owns 1.5 million barrels of oil, the convenience yield makes the holding more risky than the PV of the obligation to receive 1.5 million barrels in 3 months. The hedge would entail selling $[(1.02^{.25}) \times (1.5 \text{ million})] = 1.5074$ million barrels of oil for 3-month forward delivery. A futures position requires selling $[(1.02/1.09)^{.25} \times (1.5 \text{ million})] = 1.4753$ million barrels of oil in 3 months.

22.10)

Since

$$d_1 = \left[\frac{\ln[(25/(28(e^{-\frac{1}{2}\times.05})))]}{0.5944\sqrt{\frac{1}{2}}} + \frac{0.5944\sqrt{\frac{1}{2}}}{2}\right] = -0.000002011$$

$$\Delta = N(d_1) = N\left(\frac{\ln(S/PV(K))}{\sigma\sqrt{T}} + \frac{\sigma\sqrt{T}}{2}\right) = N(-0.000002011) = 0.4999992$$

Thus, they need to buy (2 million/0.4999992) = 4.000006 options.

22.11)

Assuming that Disney and Metallgesellschaft have about the same bargaining power, they can divide the savings equally after paying 0.4% to the bank. Let Disney borrow $20 million dollars at 6% and let Metallgesellschaft borrow €24 million at 10.0%. The bank earns 0.4% of the $20 million notional amount of the swap.

To achieve equal gains, Disney swaps its dollar-denominated 6% debt for (9.70% – 0.85%) = 8.85% € bonds while Metallgesellschaft swaps its 10% € debt for (8.40% – 0.85%) = 7.55% (US$) bonds.

	Disney	Metallgesellschaft
before swap cost of funds	9.7% (€)	8.4% (US$)
after swap cost of funds	10% (€)	6% (US$)
gain/loss	-0.3% (€)	2.4% (US$)
side payment or transfer	1.15% = 10.00% – 8.85%	−1.55% [The difference (0.4%) goes to the bank] = 6% – 7.55%
net gain/loss	0.85%	0.85%

22.12)

The company's cash flow is modeled as:

$$C = \alpha + 2 F_{int} + 5 F_{ex} + \varepsilon$$

Therefore, you must find a costless portfolio with interest rate sensitivity equal to −2 and exchange rate sensitivity equal to −5. Let:

x_1 = millions of dollars invested in 30-year government bonds
x_2 = number of $1 million contracts in the costless interest rate swap
x_3 = millions of dollars invested in the foreign index fund

The portfolio must satisfy the following constraints with regard to:

Cost: $0 = 1,000,000x_1 + 0x_2 + 1,000,000x_3$

Interest-rate sensitivity: $-2 = -4x_1 - 2x_2 - 3x_3$

Exchange-rate sensitivity: $-5 = 6x_2 - 2x_3$

Solving these equations: $x_1 = 11; x_2 = -4.5; x_3 = -11$

So the solution is to:

(1) buy $11 million in 30-year government bonds
(2) short 4.5 $1 million swap contracts
(3) short $11 million in the foreign index fund.

22.13)

a)

$$\beta \text{ per dollar invested in the factory} = \frac{-\$130\,\text{million}}{\$100\,\text{million}} = -1.3$$

Standard deviation of sales margin for 10,000 cars = $(10,000) \times (\$1,000) = \$10$ million

$$\text{Standard deviation per dollar invested in the factory} = \frac{\$10\,\text{million}}{\$100\,\text{million}} = 0.1$$

Variance per dollar invested in the factory = 0.01

Covariance between Ford's stock return and the cash flow per dollar invested in the factory:

$\beta[\text{var (Ford stock return)}] = (-1.30) \times (0.5^2) = -0.325$

Suppose the minimum variance portfolio has the fraction x invested in Ford's stock and the fraction $(1 - x)$ invested in the factory. Then:

cov(Ford stock, portfolio) = (x)var (Ford) + $(1 - x)$ cov(Ford, factory)

$$= (x)(0.25) + (1 - x)(-0.325)$$

cov(Factory, portfolio) = $(x)(-0.325) + (1 - x)(0.01)$

$0.25x + (1 - x)(-0.325) = -0.325x + (0.01)(1 - x)$

$x = 0.3681 \approx 0.37$

This implies that, if Ford has a capital constraint of $100 million to spend and the factory is scalable, then Ford should invest in a smaller factory which produces 6300 cars at a cost of $63 million and buy $37 million of Ford's stock.

b)

To identify the tangency portfolio, use equation (5.2) in chapter 5. The expected return to the factory is:

[$10,000(22,000) − $100,000,000]/$100,000,000 = 1.20.

Thus, the weights of the tangency portfolio satisfy:

$$\frac{0.30-0.10}{0.25x+(1-x)(-0.325)} = \frac{1.20-0.10}{-0.325x+(0.01)(1-x)}$$

$x = 0.5139 \approx 0.51$

If Ford has $100 million to spend and the factory is scalable, then the tangency portfolio consists of $51 million in Ford stock and a $49 million factory producing 4900 cars.

22.14)

$$\text{var}(xW + (1-x)\,E) = (x^2)(0.09) + 2x(1-x)(0.25)(0.3)(0.2) + (1-x)^2\,(0.04)$$

$$= 0.09x^2 + 0.03x - 0.03x^2 + 0.04\,(1 - 2x + x^2)$$

$$= 0.1x^2 - 0.05x + 0.04$$

So to minimize:

$$\frac{\partial \, \text{var}}{\partial x} = 0.2x - 0.05 = 0$$

$x = 0.25$

To minimize return variance, the NBA should maintain a proportion of 25% Western teams and 75% Eastern teams.

CHAPTER 23
INTEREST RATE RISK MANAGEMENT

23.1)

a)

Annually compounded yield = 8%

b)

$$\text{Duration} = \frac{\dfrac{8}{1.08} \times 1 + \dfrac{8}{(1.08)^2} \times 2 + \dfrac{108}{(1.08)^3} \times 3}{100} = 2.78 \text{ years}$$

At r = 8.00%, P = $100.00

At r = 7.99%, P = $100.0258

DV01 = $100.0258 − $100.00 = $0.0258

c)

$\Delta P = (-DV01) \times (\Delta \text{ b.p.}) = (-\$0.0258) \times (-10) = \$0.258$

If yield-to-maturity declines 10 basis points, the bond's price will increase by $0.26

23.2)

The price of the bond is represented by:

$$P = \sum_{t=1}^{T} C_t \exp(-(r + \delta)t)$$

where C_t is the cash flow at time t. Therefore:

$$\frac{dP}{d\delta} = -\sum_{t=1}^{T} tC_t \exp(-(r + \delta)t)$$

This implies:

$$-\frac{1}{P}\frac{dP}{d\delta} = \frac{1}{P}\sum_{t=1}^{T} tC_t \exp(-(r + \delta)t)$$

At $\delta = 0$, this has the value:

$$\frac{1}{P}\sum_{t=1}^{T} tC_t \exp(-rt) = (\text{present value}) \text{ Duration.}$$

23.3)

a)

Setting the DV01 of the portfolio to 0:

$$\text{DV01(portfolio)} = (\$1 \text{ million}) \left(\frac{0.10}{100}\right) + (x) \left(\frac{0.05}{100}\right) = 0$$

The solution is: $x = -\$2,000,000$.

She should short $2 million of Bond B in order to hedge all interest rate risk in the portfolio.

b)

Since these are par bonds, $P_A = 100 = P_B$. From equation (23.7a):

$\text{DV01} = (\text{DUR}) (P) (0.0001)$

$0.10 = (\text{DUR}_A) (100) (0.0001)$

$\text{DUR}_A = 10$

$0.05 = \text{DUR}_B (100) (0.0001)$

$\text{DUR}_B = 5$

To immunize the bond portfolio to a horizon of seven years, we must solve for weight x where:

$x(10 \text{ years}) + (1 - x) (5 \text{ years}) = 7 \text{ years}$

$5x = 2$

$x = 0.40$

$1 - x = 0.60$

So, to immunize the $1 million portfolio to a horizon of seven years, we should have $400,000 in Bond A and $600,000 in Bond B.

23.4)

a)

For the bond, the accrued interest is: $\dfrac{16 + 11}{184} \times 4 = \$0.5870$

For the note, the accrued interest is: $\dfrac{27}{184} \times 3.5 = \$0.5136$

b)

Setting the DV01 of the portfolio to 0:

$$\text{DV01(portfolio)} = \$1 \text{ million} \left(\frac{0.10}{100}\right) + (x) \left(\frac{0.06}{100}\right) = 0$$

$x = -\$1,666,667$.

To eliminate all interest rate risk, short $1.67 million (face value) in notes.

23.5)

a)

Since $\$90 = \dfrac{\$100}{(1+y_1)} \Rightarrow y_1 = 0.1111 = 11.11\%$

$\$80 = \dfrac{\$100}{(1+y_2)^2} \Rightarrow y_2 = .1180 = 11.80\%$

The no arbitrage price must be:

$$\dfrac{\$8}{1+y_1} + \dfrac{\$108}{(1+y_2)^2} = \dfrac{\$8}{1.1111} + \dfrac{\$108}{(1.1180)^2} = \$7.20 + \$86.41 = \$93.61$$

b)

$$\dfrac{\$7.20}{\$93.61} \times 1 + \dfrac{\$86.41}{\$93.61} \times 2 = DUR \text{ (present value)}$$

$$= 0.0769 + 1.8462 = 1.9231 \text{ years}$$

c)

The market value of a $1 million face value bond position is $ 0.9361 million.

$$\dfrac{DUR_H}{DUR_B} = \dfrac{P_B}{P_H}$$

$$\dfrac{3}{1.9231} = \dfrac{\$0.9361\,\text{million}}{P_H}$$

Therefore, $P_H = \$0.6$ million

23.6)

$$DUR = \dfrac{1}{100}\left[\dfrac{3}{1.03}\times 0.5 + \dfrac{3}{(1.03)^2}\times 1 + \dfrac{3}{(1.03)^3}\times 1.5 + \dfrac{3}{(1.03)^4}\times 2 + \dfrac{3}{(1.03)^5}\times 2.5 + \dfrac{103}{(1.03)^6}\times 3 \right]$$

$$= 2.79 \text{ years}$$

P(y=6.01%) = $99.972919; P(y=5.99%) = $100.027090

DV01(6.00%) = $100.027090 – $100 = $0.027090

DV01(6.01%) = $100 – $99.972919 = $0.027081

CONV = ($1million/P) [DV01(6.00%) – DV01(6.01%)]

= ($1million/100) [$0.027090 – $0.027081]

= 0.09

23.7)

$DUR = 1.91$ years

$P(y=6.01\%) = \$\ 99.981417$

$P(y=5.99\%) = \$100.018588$

$DV01(6.00\%) = \$100.018588 - \$100.00 = \$0.018588$

$DV01(6.01\%) = \$100.00 - \$99.981417 = \$0.018583$

$CONV = (\$1\text{million}/P) \times [DV01(6.00\%) - DV01(6.01\%)]$

$\qquad = (\$1\text{million}/100) \times [\$0.018588 - \$0.018583]$

$\qquad = 0.05$

23.8)

For a given position size, P, in the 3-year 6% bond, we can use DVO1 hedging to create a portfolio that hedges interest rate risk. Specifically, we solve for x, the position taken in the 2-year bond, that satisfies:

$P(0.027090) + x(0.018588) = 0$

$x = -1.46P$

This value represents the position taken in the 2-year bond which hedges the portfolio against interest rate risk (as measured by DVO1) for a given position size P. Thus, for every \$100 in the 3-year bond (i.e., P = \$100), we have to short \$146 in the 2-year premium bond.

23.9)

For the 10% premium bond:

$$P(y=6.00\%) = \frac{5}{1.03} + \frac{5}{1.03^2} + \frac{5}{1.03^3} + \frac{105}{1.03^4} = \$107.434197$$

$$P(y=5.99\%) = \frac{5}{\left(1+\dfrac{.0599}{2}\right)} + \frac{5}{\left(1+\dfrac{.0599}{2}\right)^2} + \frac{5}{\left(1+\dfrac{.0599}{2}\right)^3} + \frac{105}{\left(1+\dfrac{.0599}{2}\right)^4} = 107.453674$$

$DV01(6.00\%) = \$107.453674 - \$107.434197 = \$0.019477$

For a given position size, P, in the 3-year, 6% bond, we can use DV01 hedging to create a portfolio that hedges interest rate risk. Specifically, we solve for x, the position taken in the premium bond, that satisfies:

$P(0.027090) + x(0.019477) = 0$

$x = -1.39P$

This value represents the position taken in the premium bond which hedges the portfolio against interest rate risk (as measured by DV01) for a given position size P. Thus, for every \$100 investment in the 3-year, 6% bond, one has to short \$139 face amount of the 2-year premium bond.

23.10)

If the term structure of interest rates is not flat, then we would hedge against changes in the term structure by first computing the term structure DV01 for each bond, and, second, take a position in the 2-year bond that hedges against parallel shifts in the term structure. Specifically, the term structure DV01 is the change in bond price for a one basis point shift in all zero-coupon rates of all maturities for which the bond produces cash flows. These DV01s are computed for each bond, and the same analysis of solving for the position to take in the 2 year bond is conducted as in Exercises 23.8 and 23.9.